Book-Keeping
in the
Hotel and
Catering
Industry

Richard Kotas,

INTERNATIONAL TEXTBOOK COMPANY

Published by
International Textbook Company Ltd.
a member of the Blackie Group
450 Edgware Road, London W2 1EG

First published 1965
Second edition 1967
This edition 1972
Reprinted 1974
Reprinted 1977

ISBN 0 7002 0176 9

Printed in Great Britain by Butler & Tanner Ltd., Frome and London

To my sons George and Andrew

Preface to First Edition   This text book has been written primarily for students following courses in hotel-keeping and catering. It has been planned to cover the requirements of students studying for the following examinations:

(a) The Intermediate Membership Examination of the Hotel and Catering Institute;

(b) The Examination in Hotel Book-keeping and Reception of the Hotel and Catering Institute;

(c) The General Catering Diploma Examination of various technical colleges.

It is hoped that this text book will also be of value to students taking the examinations of the Institutional Management Association. Trainees and supervisors who have had no formal training in book-keeping should find the book useful.

I wish to place on record my appreciation of the assistance I have received in the writing of this book. Thanks are due:

To S. Medlik, M.A., B.Com., F.H.C.I., F.R.Econ.S., who has read Chapters 4 and 5, and made valuable suggestions on the sequencing of chapters. To J. J. Lanning, secretary of the Hotel and Catering Institute, for permission to reproduce past examination papers. To my colleague, J. T. Weston, A.C.A., who has read the proofs and commented on them. To my colleague, J. R. S. Beavis, B.A., A.C.A., who has read several chapters and made some useful suggestions. To G. N. Porter, manager, Education and Training Division of Addo Ltd; R. H. G. Walpole, manager, Hotel and Catering Systems Advisory Service of the National Cash Register Co. Ltd; D. R. Stephenson, hotels manager of Sweda Ltd; J. K. Ferguson of the Education Division of British Olivetti Ltd, for assistance with the chapter on mechanized accounting and for permission to reproduce the necessary illustrative material. To the Director of H.M. Stationery Office for permission to reproduce various official documents in connection with the chapter on wages and salaries.

Finally, various names of hotel and catering establishments are used in the examples and problems given in this book. All such names are purely fictitious and have no connection with any actual businesses in the industry which may bear the same name.

London, 1965   Richard Kotas

Preface to Second Edition

The ready acceptance of the present textbook has necessitated the printing of a second edition rather earlier than anticipated. The opportunity has been taken to correct one or two minor errors; also a section has been added on the Selective Employment Payments Tax.

Changes relating to the preparation of wages and salaries occur with such frequency that no textbook dealing with this aspect of book-keeping can long be up-to-date. The basic principles are set out in Chapter 5 but students are advised to make themselves familiar with the details of current regulations relating to P.A.Y.E., N.I.C., G.P.S., S.E.T., etc. and to note carefully any changes as they are announced officially.

London, 1967   Richard Kotas

Preface to Third Edition

The introduction of decimal currency has necessitated yet another edition of *Book-Keeping in the Hotel and Catering Industry.*

Changes relating to P.A.Y.E. and wages regulation orders have been so frequent that it has been found impossible to present up-to-date information in the previous editions. In this third edition the chapter on wages and salaries has, therefore, been omitted.

Chapter 11, entitled 'Other forms of ownership' is intended to give students a brief introduction to types of business other than the sole trader.

It is hoped that 'Book-keeping in the Hotel and Catering Industry' will continue to be of value to students in colleges, particularly those preparing for the Ordinary National Diploma in Hotel and Catering Operations.

Guildford, 1972   Richard Kotas

Contents

CHAPTER 1

Theory and mechanics of double entry

Nature of business transactions In the course of any one day, a business will make a number of transactions. It will buy provisions, wines, and spirits from its suppliers; sell meals, drinks, and accommodation to its customers; pay business expenses such as rent, rates, wages, and salaries; and buy china, cutlery, and equipment.

All such transactions result in a transfer of money (or money's worth, value, or benefit) between two parties; the giver and the recipient of value. Thus, when a hotel buys provisions from its supplier, the giver of value is the supplier and the recipient of value is the hotel. When wages are paid by the hotel, the hotel is the giver and the employees are the recipients of money. When a meal is served to a customer, the hotel is the giver and the customer the recipient of value.

Hence, it may be said that *every business transaction has two aspects: the yielding of a benefit and the receiving of that benefit*, and it is impossible to think of one without the other.

The ledger In order to have a systematic record of all transactions, it is necessary to keep what is known as the ledger. This is the principal book of account and contains a number of ledger accounts, each of which will be ruled as in Figure 1.

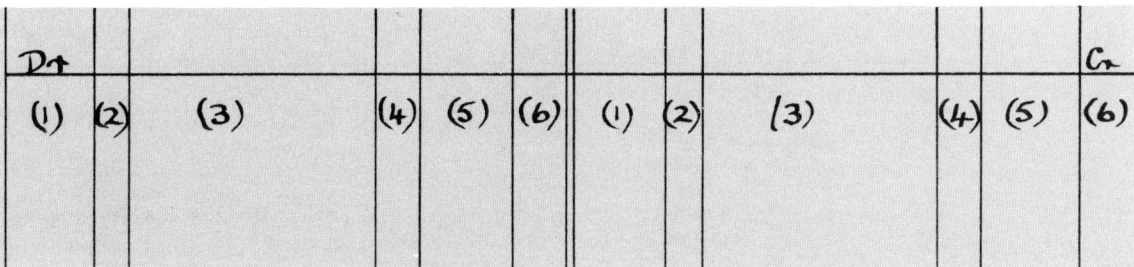

Figure 1

It will be observed that the ledger account is divided into two identical parts. The left-hand side of the account is known as the *debit side* (abbreviated to Dr.), and the right-hand side of the account is known as the *credit side* (abbreviated to Cr.).

The columns numbered (1)—(6) are used as follows:

(1) The month;
(2) the day of the month;
(3) particulars;
(4) folio (a folio is a page in a book of account; the pages of the ledger are numbered consecutively and each ledger account appears on a different page; the folio column is used to cross-reference the double entry of a transaction);
(5)–(6) money columns for pounds and pence respectively.

***Principle of double
entry***

In order to have a complete record of all transactions, each transaction must be entered in the ledger twice: once on the debit and once on the credit side of an account. The receiving of value is entered on the debit side and the giving of value on the credit side, as in Figure 2.

Dr											Cr
	VALUE RECEIVED						VALUE GIVEN				

Figure 2

The following examples show how the principle of double entry is applied in the recording of transactions.

(a) On 1st January, 19 . ., a hotel pays wages of £100.

Dr 19..			Wages A/c							Cr
Jan	1	Cash	100	00						

Dr			Cash A/c			19..				Cr
						Jan	1	Wages	100	00

Figure 3

Note: The cash account of the hotel has given value and is, therefore, credited; the wages account (representing the employees) has received value and is, therefore, debited.

(b) On 4th February, 19 . ., a restaurant borrows £1 000 from X Finance Company.

Dr 19..			Cash A/c							Cr
Feb	4	X Finance Co.	1 000	00						

			X Finance Co A/c			19..				Cr.
						Feb	4	Cash	1 000	00

Figure 4

Note: The cash account of the restaurant has taken value and is therefore debited; the finance company has given value to the restaurant and is therefore credited.

(c) On 3rd April, 19.., a motel buys furniture on credit from Motel Furnishers Limited for £500.

Dr			Furniture A/c							Cr	
19..											
Apr	3	Motel Furn. Ltd	500	00							
			Motel Furnishers Ltd. A/c							Cr	
					19..						
					Apr	3	Furniture			500	00

Figure 5

Note: The suppliers of furniture have given value and their account in the ledger must be credited accordingly; the corresponding debit entry must therefore be in the furniture account of the motel.

(d) On 7th September, 19.., a hotel receives rent of £50 in respect of sub-let premises.

Dr			Cash A/c							Cr	
19..											
Sept	7	Rent Receivable	50	00							
Dr			Rent Receivable A/c							Cr	
					19..						
					Sept	7	Cash			50	00

Figure 6

Note: The cash account of the hotel, having received value, is debited; the corresponding credit entry must therefore be made in the rent receivable account.

A consideration of the examples given will show that:

(1) By applying the principle of double entry it is possible to ensure that *both aspects of each transaction* are reflected in the books of a business;
(2) a separate account is used for every type of transaction; as a result, at the end of any one period the ledger contains *a systematic and classified summary* of all the transactions for the period concerned; and
(3) as there is a debit and a credit entry in respect of each transaction, *the sum total of debit entries must be equal to the sum total of the credit entries in the ledger.*

A second illustration is given below, showing how the principle of double entry is applied within a particular business.

On 1st March, 19. ., A. Caterer started in business with a capital in cash of £5 000. During March his transactions were as follows:

March	2	Paid quarterly rent	£250
,,	4	Purchased furniture for cash	500
,,	6	Bought equipment on credit from H. and C. Ltd	300
,,	8	Paid wages	50
,,	11	Bought provisions on credit from B. Blake & Son	100
,,	14	Sold meals for cash	75
,,	18	Paid wages	60
,,	22	Sold meals for cash	45
,,	26	Paid wages	65
,,	29	Paid H. and C. Ltd	100
,,	31	Sold meals for cash	30

(a) A. Caterer's transactions to be entered in his ledger.
(b) The accuracy of the ledger entries to be checked as at 31st March, 19. . .

Dr   **Cash A/c**   **Cr**

19..					19..				
Mar	1	Capital	5000	00	Mar	2	Rent	250	00
"	14	Sales	75	00	"	4	Furniture	500	00
"	22	– do –	45	00	"	8	Wages	50	00
"	31	– do –	30	00	"	18	– do –	60	00
					"	26	– do –	65	00
					"	29	H & C Ltd	100	00

Dr   **Capital A/c**   **Cr**

					19..				
					Mar	1	Cash	5000	00

Dr   **Rent A/c**   **Cr**

19..				
Mar	2	Cash	250	00

Dr   **Furniture A/c**   **Cr**

19..				
Mar	4	Cash	500	00

Dr			Equipment A/c							Cr	
19..											
Mar	6	H & C Ltd		300	00						

Dr			H & C Ltd A/c							Cr	
19..						19..					
Mar	29	Cash		100	00	Mar	6	Equipment		300	00

Dr			Wages A/c							Cr	
19..											
Mar	8	Cash		50	00						
"	18	– do –		60	00						
"	26	– do –		65	00						

Dr			Purchases A/c							Cr	
19..											
Mar	11	B. Blake & Son		100	00						

Dr			B. Blake & Son A/c							Cr	
						19..					
						Mar	11	Purchases		100	00

Dr			Sales A/c							Cr	
						19..					
						Mar	14	Cash		75	00
						"	22	– do –		45	00
						"	31	– do –		30	00

Figure 7

The most important check of the accuracy of the entries in the ledger is the agreement of the total of debit entries with the total of credit entries. In order to find out whether or not there is this agreement, it is necessary to extract what is known as *the trial balance*. This is done by extracting a list of ledger accounts, showing the total of the debit entries and the total of the credit entries in each account, as follows:

Trial balance as at 31st March, 19..

	Dr. £	Cr. £
Cash account	5 150	1 025
Capital account		5 000
Rent account	250	
Furniture account	500	
Equipment account	300	
H. and C. Ltd account	100	300
Wages account	175	
Purchases account	100	
B. Blake & Son account		100
Sales account		150
	£6 575	£6 575

In practice, instead of showing the total of the debit side and the total of the credit side of an account only the difference between the two sides is shown. Thus, whether we show that the H. and C. Ltd account has a debit total of £100 and a credit total of £300 or show the difference, i.e. £200, in the credit column of the trial balance has no effect on its agreement. We would thus re-write our trial balance as follows:

Trial balance as at 31st March, 19..

	Dr. £	Cr. £
Cash account	4 125	
Capital account		5 000
Rent account	250	
Furniture account	500	
Equipment account	300	
H. and C. Ltd account		200
Wages account	175	
Purchases account	100	
B. Blake & Son account		100
Sales account		150
	£5 450	£5 450

Balancing: nature of balances The difference between the two sides of an account is known as the *balance*. A *debit balance* arises when the total of debit entries exceeds the total of credit entries. A *credit balance* arises when the total of credit entries exceeds the total of debit entries.

The method of balancing the account is shown below.

Dr			Cash A/c						Cr	
19..					19..					
Jan	1	Capital	2 000	00	Jan	4	Rent		300	00
"	16	Sales	200	00	"	9	China		200	00
"	29	– do –	300	00	"	14	Wages		200	00
					"	31	Furniture		1 000	00
						31	Balance	c/d	800	00
			2 500	00					2 500	00
19..										
Feb	1	Balance	b/d 800	00						

Figure 8

Note: It will be observed that:

(a) The total of the debit entries in the cash account is £2 500 and the total of the credit entries £1 700, giving a debit balance of £800.

(b) In order to balance the cash account (i.e. make both sides of the account equal) it is necessary to place the balance on the credit side of the account.

(c) Both money columns are then totalled and the balance is entered as the figure brought down on the debit side.

The abbreviations c/d and b/d stand for 'carried down' and 'brought down', respectively. When a balance is carried from one page of the ledger to another or from one accounting period to another it is said to be 'carried forward', hence the abbreviations c/f and b/f are then used.

A debit balance may represent one of two things. It may be an asset, e.g. furniture, china, cash, etc., or an expense (or loss), e.g. wages, rent, purchases. Similarly, a credit balance may represent one of two things. It may be a liability, e.g. an amount owing to suppliers, or a gain (or income) such as sales, as is indicated in the chart below.

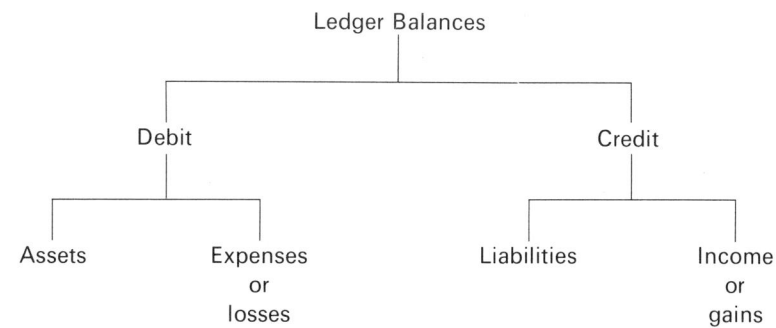

The main purpose of the present chapter is to explain and illustrate the principle of double entry. In the next few chapters we will consider the more practical aspects of book-keeping, an important feature of which is the keeping of books other than, and subsidiary to, the ledger.

Problems

1 Explain what is meant by the principle of double entry.

2 What do you understand by: (a) the ledger; (b) debit balance; (c) credit balance?

3 From the following information, write up V. Goodfellow's cash account and balance it as at 7th March, 19 . .:

March 1	Balance b/d	Dr. £3 152
,, 1	Received from B. Smythe	26
,, 2	Paid rent	550
,, 3	Paid for stationery	13
,, 4	Sold meals for cash	312
,, 4	Paid wages	166
,, 5	Paid Hotel Suppliers Ltd	200
,, 6	Paid electricity account	96
,, 6	Sold meals for cash	327
,, 7	Paid Wm. Grocer & Sons	55
,, 7	Paid for advertising	22

4 On 1st January, 19 . ., J. Robinson started as a café proprietor with a capital in cash of £5 000. His transactions in January were:

January 1	Purchased premises for cash	£3 000
,, 3	Paid for kitchen utensils and equipment	250
,, 5	Paid for furniture	375
,, 10	Paid wages	37
,, 12	Purchased provisions for cash	125
,, 14	Sold meals, etc., for cash	56
,, 16	Paid insurance	20
,, 18	Paid wages	39
,, 19	Sold meals, etc., for cash	63
,, 21	Bought provisions on credit from M. Mann & Co.	35
,, 23	Paid for cleaning materials	12
,, 25	Paid wages	38
,, 27	Sold meals, etc., for cash	45
,, 29	Purchased provisions for cash	27
,, 31	Purchased additional equipment for cash	100

Enter the above transactions in Robinson's ledger, extract a trial balance as at 31st January, 19 . ., and balance his cash account.

5 On 1st July, 19 . ., W. Gravett started in business as a snack bar proprietor with a capital in cash of £100. His transactions in July were:

July 1	Borrowed £2 000 from City Finance Co.
,, 5	Bought premises for £6 000 and settled the purchase price as follows: paid a deposit of £500 and obtained a mortgage for the balance due (£5 500) from the Stable Building Society.
,, 9	Purchased furniture on credit for £750 from Oak Furnishing Company.
,, 13	Paid in cash £600 for china and equipment.
,, 18	Bought provisions on credit from B. Baker & Sons for £80, and from S. Fish & Company for £95.
,, 24	Sold meals for cash £105.
,, 28	Paid wages £50.
,, 29	Sold meals on credit to Midland Motors Ltd £50, and B.M. Dining Club £75.
,, 30	Borrowed from A. Lender £500.
,, 31	Paid Oak Furnishing Company £50.

Enter Gravett's transactions in his ledger, extract a trial balance as at 31st July, 19 . ., and balance the cash account.

CHAPTER 2

Accounting for cash

Due to the varying circumstances of each business it will be found that the actual arrangement and layout of books of account vary somewhat from one business to another. We thus find many kinds of cash accounts (cash books, as they are usually called).

Single column cash book

This is the simplest form of cash book and has already been illustrated in Chapter 1. It takes the form of a ledger account. The debit side is used for the recording of money (coin, notes, cheques, postal orders, travellers' cheques, etc.) received; the credit side is used for money paid.

Example

The following cash transactions are to be recorded in the cash book of the Milano Restaurant; the cash book balanced and the balance brought down as at 31st January, 19..:

January	1	Debit balance b/d	£1 000
,,	2	Paid wages	125
,,	7	Cash sales	420
,,	11	Paid to A. Supplier	45
,,	16	Received from B. Brown	80
,,	21	Paid wages	125
,,	26	Cash sales	430
,,	31	Paid for linen	30

19..						19..				
Jan	1	Balance	b/d	1 000 00	Jan	2	Wages		125 00
,,	7	Cash Sales		420 00	,,	11	A. Supplier		45 00
,,	16	B. Brown		80 00	,,	21	Wages		125 00
,,	26	Cash Sales		430 00	,,	31	Linen		30 00
					,,	31	Balance	c/d	1 605 00
				1 930 00					1 930 00
19..									
Feb	1	Balance	b/d	1 605 00					

Figure 9

Double column cash book

Consideration of the single column cash book will indicate that it is inadequate in some respects. First, the majority of businesses keep most of their cash in a bank account and some 'office cash' on the premises. Second, though some payments are made by cheque others are in cash. Hence it is necessary to have a cash book which will distinguish between the two separate funds of cash (i.e. bank account and office cash) and thus differentiate between payments made by cheque and those in actual cash.

The double column cash book has two money columns, headed 'cash' and 'bank', on the debit side, and two money columns, also headed 'cash' and 'bank', on the credit side. The cash and bank columns are used as follows:

Debit side All amounts paid into office cash are entered in the 'cash' column and all amounts banked in the 'bank' column.

Credit side All amounts paid out of office cash are entered in the 'cash' column and all payments by cheque in the 'bank' column.

Any amounts of cash transferred from the bank to the office should be credited in the bank column and debited in the cash column; any transfers of cash from the office to the bank should be credited in the cash column and debited in the bank column. Any transfer of cash from the bank to the office, or *vice versa*, is shown in the cash book by means of a 'contra entry'. The term contra entry means that both the debit and the credit entry are to be found in the same account; contra entries are denoted by the sign ¢.

Example The following transactions are to be entered in the cash book of the Chelsea Luncheon Club, and the cash book balanced as at 28th February, 19 . .:

February	1	Bank balance b/d	Dr. £2 000
,,	1	Balance of office cash b/d	20
,,	2	Paid by cheque for furniture	250
,,	4	Paid by cheque to A. B. Manning	45
,,	5	Paid for stamps — cash	3
,,	7	Banked cash sales	215
,,	9	Paid wages by cheque	82
,,	11	Paid by cheque H.C.I. Supplies Ltd	115
,,	13	Received from B. Naylor and banked	25
,,	15	Paid manager's travelling expenses — cash	6
,,	18	Banked cash sales	245
,,	20	Paid wages by cheque	92
,,	22	Paid for stationery — cash	5
,,	23	Paid for flowers — cash	2
,,	24	Withdrew from bank for office use	20
,,	25	Banked cash sales	190
,,	26	Paid by cheque to M. Cooper & Sons	65
,,	27	Paid for stamps — cash	3
,,	27	Paid cleaner's wages — cash	5
,,	28	Paid wages by cheque	86

Cash Book

Date		F	CASH	BANK	Date		F	CASH	BANK
19..		b/d			19..				
Feb. 1	Balances		20	2,000	Feb. 2	Furniture			250
" 7	Cash Sales			215	" 4	A.B. Manning			45
" 13	B. Naylor			25	" 5	Stamps		3	
" 18	Cash Sales			245	" 9	Wages			82
" 24	Bank	¢	20		" 11	H·C·I·Supplies Ltd			115
" 25	Cash Sales			190	" 15	Manager's Trav. Exp.		6	
					" 20	Wages			92
					" 22	Stationery		5	
					" 23	Flowers		2	
					" 24	Cash	¢		20
					" 26	M. Cooper & Sons			65
					" 27	Stamps		3	
					" 27	Cleaner's Wages		5	
					" 28	Wages			86
					" 28	Balances	c/d	16	1920
			40	2675				40	2675
19..		b/d							
Mar. 1	Balances		16	1920					

Figure 10

Petty cash book In hotel and catering establishments it is often necessary to make numerous payments of small amounts for various expenses. Where this is so, it may be convenient to have a main cash book and a separate petty cash book. The main cash book would be in the charge of a senior clerk or the head cashier, whereas the responsibility for maintaining the petty cash book would be delegated to a relatively junior clerk.

Petty cash books are usually analysed and kept on what is known as the *imprest system*. This operates as follows. At the beginning of a period a fixed amount of cash, say £20, is advanced to the petty cashier. At the end of the period the petty cashier balances his petty cash book, and the total amount expended by him (and represented by appropriate vouchers) is refunded to him by the person in charge of the main cash book. Thus, at the beginning of each period, the petty cashier will start with the same fixed float of cash.

For example:

	£
Petty cashier's cash float on 1st January, 19..	20
,, ,, weekly expenditure (total vouchers)	16
,, ,, balance of cash on 7th January, 19..	4
Therefore (i) cash refunded to him on 7th January, 19..	16
(ii) his cash float on 8th January, 19..	£20

Example   The petty cash book of the Wessex Hotel is kept on the imprest system. On 1st July, 19.., the petty cashier's balance is £20. His expenditure during the first week of July was:

July 1	Paid for postage stamps	£2.25
,, 2	Paid for guest's telegram (Room 64)—Jones	0.75
,, 3	Paid manager's fares	2.75
,, 3	Bought flowers for guest (Room 87)—Brown	1.50
,, 4	Paid for postage stamps	1.75
,, 5	Gave tip to delivery man	0.25
,, 5	Bought bill pads for restaurant	2.50
,, 6	Paid chef's fares	0.75
,, 7	Paid donation to local charity	0.50
,, 7	Bought pencils and ink	0.25

The above payments should be recorded and, assuming that the total of expenditure is refunded, the petty cash book balanced as at 7th July, 19...

It will be observed that every petty cash payment is recorded twice: once in the total column and once in one of the analysis columns: consequently, the sum of the analysed totals should be equal to that of the total column.

In the folio column are recorded the numbers of the petty cash vouchers. These would be numbered consecutively and presented to the head cashier when requesting a refund in respect of payments made.

V.P.O. stands for 'visitors' paid outs'. This is a column often added in the petty cash book of a hotel. Payments made on behalf of guests staying in the hotel are recorded in this column. As soon as a payment of this kind is made, a copy of the appropriate voucher should be passed on to the reception office (bill office, in a larger hotel) to ensure that the charge is debited to the guest's account in the visitors' ledger. In many hotels the total of V.P.O. from the petty cash book is checked against the total of debits in the V.P.O. column of the visitors' ledger to ensure that all charges have been posted.

The petty cash book, though physically separated from the ledger, is a ledger account: as a result, every entry made in it counts for double entry purposes. It is also *a subsidiary book* in that it collects and analyses detailed transactions and enables totals to be posted to the ledger.

PETTY CASH BOOK
16

Dr		Date			F	Total		Postage		Stationery		Travelling Exp		V.P.O		Sundry Exp	
20	00	July 1	Balance		b/d												
		" 1	Postage Stamps		1	2	25	2	25								
		" 2	Guest's Telegram Rm 64 – Jones		2		75								75		
		" 3	Manager's Fares		3	2	75					2	75				
		" 3	Guest's Flowers Rm 87 – Brown		4	1	50							1	50		
		" 4	Postage Stamps		5	1	75	1	75								
		" 5	Tip to Delivery Man		6		25										25
		" 5	Bill Pads		7	2	50			2	50						
		" 6	Chef's Fares		8		75						75				
		" 7	Donation to Charity		9		50										50
		" 7	Pencils and Ink		10		25				25						
						13	25	4	00	2	75	3	50	2	25		75
		" 7	Balance		c/d	6	75	L/29		L/31		L/45				L/47	
20	00					20	00										
6	75	July 8	Balance		b/d												
13	25	" 8	Cash Received														

Figure 11

13

Double entry in respect of petty cash items is completed as follows:

(a) Any amounts drawn by the petty cashier are credited in the main cash book and debited in the petty cash book.

(b) Petty cash payments are credited (individually) in the petty cash book and debited in total in the appropriate account in the ledger. Thus the total of the postage column, £4, would be debited in the postage account as in Figure 12.

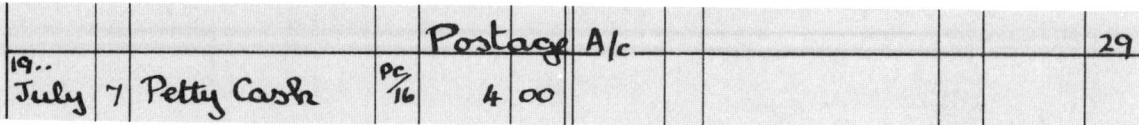

Figure 12

Note that the totals posted to the ledger are cross-referenced as follows:

(a) Under the analysis totals of the petty cash book the page number of the relevant ledger account is given. In the illustration, L/29 means that the corresponding double entry is in the postage account which is on page 29 in the ledger. The ledger folio column shows the relevant page number of the petty cash book.

(b) The V.P.O. items, as already explained, are debited individually in the visitors' ledger. Hence the total of the V.P.O. column is left in the petty cash book.

Treatment of discounts received

Many suppliers of hotel and catering establishments offer cash discounts. A cash discount is a deduction allowed from the amount due to the supplier, provided that payment is made within a specified time. Thus, if a hotel owes A. Supplier £100, and the latter allows a discount of five per cent, provided that the payment is made within the specified time £5 may be deducted from the amount due, and only £95 need be paid. It may be seen, therefore, that the main object of cash discounts is to encourage prompt payment.

In order to facilitate the recording of cash discounts received, many hotel and catering establishments add a discount received column on the credit side of their cash book. The layout of a cash book with a discount received column is illustrated in Figure 13.

Cash Book.

Date		F	Detail	Bank	Date		F	Discount Received	Bank
19.. Jan 1	Balance	b/d		1200 00	19.. Jan 3	Wages			220 00
" 2	Sales:				" 4	A. Supplier	L/45	5 00	95 00
	Restaurant		200 00		" 4	X. Tobacco Co.		10 00	220 00
	Bar		120 00		" 5	Rent			350 00
	Sundries		20 00	340 00	" 6	Insurance			30 00

Figure 13

The discount received column is described as a memorandum column. It is there for convenience and does not count for double entry purposes. Double entry in respect of discounts received is completed as follows. Debit both the cash paid and the discount received in the account of the supplier. Credit the periodical (usually monthly) total of the discount received column in the discount received account in the ledger.

Assuming that the total of discounts received from suppliers by the end of January, 19. ., is £50, the entry in the discount received account would be:

Discount Received A/c

						19..					
						Jan	31	Cash	CB/22	50	00

Figure 14

The amount paid to A. Supplier would be posted to his account as in Figure 15.

A. Supplier A/c — 45

19..						19..					
Jan	4	Cash	CB/22	95	00	Jan	1	Balance	b/d	100	00
"	4	Discount	CB/22	5	00						
				100	00					100	00

Figure 15

The purpose of the detail column on the debit side of the cash book is twofold: to indicate the sources of any cash banked, and to facilitate an easy cross-reference to the ledger account concerned.

Cash received book

Many hotels maintain, in addition to the main cash book, a cash received book. This is kept in the reception office and usually acts as a subsidiary book to the main cash book. A typical cash received book is illustrated in Figure 16.

Date	Name	Rm. No. or Fol.	Visitors Led. Receipts		Sales Led. Receipts		Deposits on Arrival		Total	
19.. May 1	R. W. Brown, Mr	Rm 106	22	60					22	60
" 1	Midland Motors Ltd.	S.L.56			18	50			18	50
" 1	A. V. Ewing, Mr. & Mrs	Rm. 117	8	50					8	50
" 1	S. P. Browning, Miss	Rm. 36	10	00			10	00		
	etc									
" 1	Total Trans. to Cash Book	CB 46	220	50	100	25	20	00	340	75

Figure 16

At the end of each day the cash received book would be balanced and the total of cash received debited in the main cash book, as shown in Figure 17.

The corresponding credit entries would be made as indicated below:

Visitors' ledger receipts—the individual amounts received from visitors would be credited in their accounts in the visitors' ledger.

Sales ledger receipts—these, again, would be credited individually in the relevant customers' accounts in the sales ledger.

CASH

| Date | | F | SALES | | | | | | | | BANK | |
			Meals		Bars		Tobaccos		Sundries			
19... Jan 1	Balance	b/d									300	10
" 2	Sales		200	00	100	00	10	25	10	75	321	00
" 3	—do—		220	00	80	10	15	10	5	05	320	25
" 4	—do—		190	20	90	80	20	00	10	00	311	00

Figure 18

Deposits on arrival—any such deposits received would be credited in the guests' accounts in the visitors' ledger on their departure.

Date		F	Detail	Bank	Date		F	Discount Received	Bank
19.. May 1	Cash Received								
	Visitors Ledger	CRB 21	220 50						
	Sales ..	CRB 21	100 25						
	Dep. on Arrival	CRB 21	20 00	340 75					

Cash Book 46

Figure 17

Multi-column cash book

Many hotel and catering establishments, particularly canteens and clubs, keep multi-column cash books. The main purpose of a multi-column cash book is to analyse, under appropriate headings, all receipts and payments and, in this way, facilitate the preparation of final accounts, as shown in Figure 18.

A multi-column cash book is particularly useful in smaller businesses, many of which do not keep a full set of books. In such circumstances the analysis columns for receipts and payments accumulate data which may be used in the preparation of final accounts.

BOOK

	F	PURCHASES				WAGES &	OTHER	BANK	
		Food	Drink	Tobaccos	Sundries	SALARIES	EXPENSES		
Supplies Co.				30 10	10 40			40	50
Brown e Sons		50 00						50	00
ern Supplies Co.			100 30					100	30
ges						250 25		250	25

Kinds of bank accounts

Reference has already been made to *the* bank account. In fact, there are two kinds of bank account that may be opened by a business: a current account and a deposit account.

A current account is an account into which payments are made and on which cheques are drawn. The balance of a current account will, therefore, vary continually.

A deposit account is an account into which money is paid with the intention of leaving it in the bank for a period of time.

The main differences between a current account and a deposit account are:

(1) Withdrawals from a current account may be made at any time, but (usually two weeks') notice of intention to withdraw from a deposit account must be given to the bank.

(2) Interest is paid by the bank on the balance standing to the credit of a deposit account; no interest is allowed in the case of a current account.

(3) Unlike a current account, a deposit account cannot be drawn upon by means of a cheque. The usual procedure is to write a letter (signed by the persons authorized to withdraw funds) to the bank informing the bank of the intention to withdraw funds from a deposit account.

Transactions affecting the current account are recorded in the bank columns of the main cash book. Any amounts lodged with the bank will be debited in the bank column; any payments by cheque will, of course, be credited in the bank column.

Before any amount is paid into a current account particulars of the cash to be banked must be entered in a *paying-in book* supplied by the bank. This usually consists of a number of paying-in slips bound together in book form. The bank cashier detaches one copy and keeps it; the other copy of the paying-in slip, having been stamped and initialled by the cashier, remains in the book for reference. A specimen paying-in slip is shown in Figure 19.

Figure 19

Any amounts transferred from a current account to a deposit account will be credited in the main cash book and debited in a deposit account opened in the ledger. Any amounts withdrawn from the deposit account will be credited in that account and debited in some other account.

Example On 1st February, 19.., the main cash book of the Bryton Hotel shows a debit balance of £3 752. On that day the amount of £1 500 is transferred to a deposit account opened by the hotel. This will be recorded as in Figure 20.

				Cash	Book							37
19.. Feb	1	Balance	b/d	3752	00	19.. Feb	1	Deposit A/c	L 59	1500	00	
				Deposit	A/c							59
19.. Feb	1	Cash	CB 37	1500	00							

Figure 20

On 15th November, 19.., £1 400 is withdrawn from the deposit account to pay for new kitchen plant. The necessary entries will then be: Cr. deposit account and Dr. kitchen plant account as shown in Figure 21.

				Deposit	A/c							59
19.. Feb	1	Cash	CB 37	1500	00	19.. Nov	15	Kitchen Plant	L 87	1400	00	
				Kitchen	Plant	A/c						87
19.. Nov	15	Deposit A/c	L 59	1400	00							

Figure 21

Cheques Bankers supply two forms of cheques:
(1) Bearer cheques—a bearer cheque is worded: 'Pay ...... or Bearer' and would be paid to the person presenting the cheque. Bearer cheques are not as safe as order cheques and are, therefore, used infrequently.

(2) Order cheques—an order cheque is worded: 'Pay ...... or Order' and is payable to a specified person or to such person as the payee may order to receive the money. A specimen of an order cheque is shown in Figure 22.

19

> *16ᵗʰ May* 19 72
>
> ## EASTMINSTER BANK LIMITED
>
> ### 13, GREEN LANE, CHISWICK, W.4.
>
> Pay *Catering Suppliers Ltd.*   or Order
>
> *One hundred pounds*   £ 100 – 50
>
> ~~*fifty pence.*~~
>
> *John Brown*
>
> A
> X 366735

Figure 22

The parties to the cheque are:
Drawer—the person who signs the cheque (John Brown)
Drawee—the banker on whom the cheque is drawn (Eastminster Bank Limited)
Payee—the person to whom the cheque is payable (Catering Suppliers Ltd)

A cheque which is not crossed is known as an *open cheque*, and cash may be obtained for it from the banker on whom it is drawn. In practice, in order to secure a measure of protection against fraud, nearly all cheques are *crossed cheques*. A crossed cheque has two parallel lines drawn across the face of it. Sometimes the words 'and Co.' are written between the lines, but they are not essential to the crossing. When a cheque is crossed the banker will not pay cash over the counter. The payee must hand the cheque to his own banker who will collect it for him and credit his account.

Crossings   A general crossing consists of two parallel lines with or without (i) the words 'and Co.', (ii) 'not negotiable'.

A special crossing consists of the name of the banker written across the face of the cheque with or without (i) the parallel lines, (ii) the words 'not negotiable'. The effect of a special crossing is to instruct the paying banker to pay only the banker named in the crossing. If a banker disobeys a crossing, he becomes liable to the true owner of the cheque for any loss caused thereby.

We must now explain what is meant by the *negotiability* of a cheque. A cheque is, in legal language, a 'negotiable instrument'. Therefore, if it is accepted by a person in exchange for value given, and in good faith, it becomes his property; his title to it cannot be disputed, provided that there is no previous forgery on it.

When a cheque is crossed 'not negotiable', it ceases to be a negotiable instrument. A person who takes a cheque so marked, takes it subject to all defects of the title of the person who gave it to him. If there is any irregularity of title, the drawer may refuse to honour the cheque and the holder of it will lose the money.

Sometimes cheques have to be *endorsed*. To endorse a cheque means to sign one's name on the back of it. Before the Cheques Act of 17th October, 1957, all order cheques had to be endorsed by the payee before being negotiated or cashed. The present position is as follows.

Endorsement is necessary in the following cases:
(a) Cheques cashed or exchanged across the counter.
(b) Cheques tendered for the credit of an account other than that of the ostensible payee.
(c) Cheques payable to joint payees; these will require endorsement if tendered for the credit of an account to which all are not parties.

Endorsement is not necessary in the following cases:
(a) Cheques paid in for the credit of the account of the payee.
(b) Cheques paid in for the credit of a joint or partnership account.

Cheques are sometimes 'dishonoured' (returned by the banker unpaid) for various reasons, e.g. in the event of the drawer's death or bankruptcy, or where there are insufficient funds to meet the cheque. The bank will attach a slip to a cheque so returned. This is usually marked R/D (refer to drawer) and really means that there are insufficient funds to pay the cheque. When a cheque is returned for some technical reason the bank will usually indicate this by means of an appropriate wording, e.g. 'words and figures differ'; 'another signature required'; 'signature differs'; 'endorsement irregular'.

Banks refuse to cash a cheque more than six months old; the cheque is then said to be a 'stale cheque'.

Bank reconciliation statements

Periodically, usually once a month, a business will receive a loose-leaf statement from its bank. This will show the balance of cash at the beginning of the period, any amounts paid in or withdrawn, and the balance of cash at the end of the period. The bank statement is a copy of the customer's account in the books of the bank and, in theory, should contain entries identical with those in the cash book of the business. In practice, it will be found that the balance shown by the bank statement and that in the cash book rarely agree, since:

(a) Cheques sent to suppliers and credited in the cash book may not have been presented for payment, and will not appear on the bank statement.

(b) Cheques, etc., received, debited in the cash book, and paid into the bank account may not have been credited by the bank.

(c) The bank statement may contain items which do not appear in the cash book, e.g. bank charges, interest, or standing orders.

(d) Errors may have arisen in either the cash book or (which is less likely) in the bank statement.

As the two balances rarely agree, it is usual to reconcile them by drawing up what is known as a bank reconciliation statement. Before this is done, it is usual to examine the bank statement and enter in the cash book all items of bank charges, interest, and standing orders. The bank reconciliation is then prepared and the cash book balanced.

Example   Figure 23 shows the cash book of the Crown Hotel Ltd.

Cash Book

Date		F	Bank	Date		F	CHQ. No.	Bank
19.. Jan 1	Balance	b/d	1000	19.. Jan 2	Properties Ltd.		501	220
" 6	Sales		150	" 8	H & C Ltd.		502	50
" 11	—do—		200	" 9	B. Browne Co.		503	80
" 24	—do—		180	" 14	H.H. Smith		504	110
				" 19	V. May & Co.		505	30
				" 27	A.S. Foods Ltd.		506	40
				" 29	W. Cramer		507	60
				" 30	A. Grocer & Co		508	50

Figure 23

At the end of the period the bank statement in Figure 24 is received.

The bank reconciliation statement of the hotel would be prepared on the following lines.

The cash book shows a debit balance of £890 (the difference between the Dr. and Cr. totals of the cash book). An examination of the bank statement shows bank

| | Crown Hotel Ltd. 17, Hill Lane, W.5 | | in Account with EASTMINSTER BANK LTD. 13, Uphill Drive, W.5 | | |

DATE	FOR CUSTOMER'S USE		DEBITS	CREDITS	BALANCE
19..					
1 JAN					1000
5 JAN		501	220		780
6 JAN				150	930
10 JAN		502	50		880
11 JAN				200	1080
16 JAN		504	110		970
24 JAN				180	1150
29 JAN		506	40		1110
31 JAN		507	60		1050
31 JAN		CH	5		1045

ABBREVIATIONS:	CB—Cheque Book Stamps	IN — Interest
	CH—Charges or Commission	SO — Standing Order

Figure 24

charges of £5. This would have to be credited in the cash book and debited in the bank charges account in the ledger. The cash book balance would thus be reduced to £885.

The next step is to reconcile the two balances, £885 and £1 045, i.e. to explain how the difference has arisen. This may be done by starting with the cash book balance and arriving at the balance per bank statement or *vice versa*. The second alternative will now be used.

Bank reconciliation statement as at 31st January, 19..

Balance per bank statement dated 31.1.19..			£1 045
Add Bank charges			5
			£1 050
Less Unpresented cheques:			
B. Brown & Co. — 503		£80	
V. May & Co. — 505		30	
A. Grocer & Co. — 508		50	160
Cash book balance as at above date			£890

Had the bank charges been deducted from the cash book balance before drawing up the bank reconciliation statement, the latter would have been done as follows:

Bank reconciliation statement as at 31st January, 19. .

Balance per bank statement dated 31.1.19. .			£1 045
Less Unpresented cheques:			
B. Brown & Co. — 503		£80	
V. May & Co. — 505		30	
A. Grocer & Co. — 508		50	160
Cash book balance as at above date			£885

Problems

1 Explain what you understand by the 'imprest system' as applied to the petty cash book. Give a specimen ruling of a petty cash book with five analysis columns.

2 B. A. Branson commenced business as a snack bar proprietor. His capital on 1st January, 19. ., consisted of:

Cash at bank	£3 980
Cash in hand	20
	£4 000

The following were Branson's transactions in January:

January	1	Paid by cheque for provisions	£40
,,	2	Paid by cheque for:	
		cash register	120
		furniture	360
		kitchen utensils	260
,,	4	Bought provisions, paid by cheque	50
,,	6	Banked cash sales	75
,,	8	Cash payments:	
		cleaning materials	4
		stationery	5
		travelling expenses	1
,,	14	Banked cash sales	30
,,	16	Paid wages, by cheque	45
,,	18	Paid by cheque for provisions	110
,,	21	Cash payments:	
		stationery	2
		vegetables	3
		postage stamps	2
,,	23	Banked cash sales	85

,,	24	Withdrew from bank for office use	20
,,	26	**Paid water rates by cheque**	30
,,	27	Paid wages by cheque	42
,,	28	Banked cash sales	35
,,	30	Paid for advertising by cheque	56
,,	31	Paid window cleaner in cash	4

Enter the above transactions in Branson's double column cash book, post to ledger, and extract his trial balance as at 31st January, 19. . .

3 Design a petty cash book to show expenditure under the headings of postage and stationery; travelling expenses; provisions; and miscellaneous expenses.

Enter the following in your petty cash book and balance it as at 6th June, 19. . .

June 1	Balance b/d		£20.00
,,	1	Bought postage stamps	2.77
,,	2	Paid messenger's fares	0.27
,,	2	Bought envelopes	0.56
,,	3	Paid for flowers	1.62
,,	3	Paid chef's fares	2.88
,,	4	Paid tip to delivery man	0.13
,,	4	Paid for coffee	0.98
,,	5	Paid for telegram	1.06
,,	5	Paid for strawberries	1.82
,,	6	Paid for blotting paper	0.17
,,	6	Bought cleaning materials	1.98

4 Explain how double entry is completed in respect of discounts received from suppliers.

5 Explain the difference between a current account and a deposit account.

6 Write short explanatory notes on each of the following: bearer cheque; order cheque; open cheque; crossed cheque; general crossing; and special crossing.

7 Explain the position with regard to the endorsement of cheques.

8 What is the object of a bank reconciliation statement? Draw up a bank reconciliation statement from the following information.

Cash book balance as at 31.3.19. .	£441
Bank statement ,, ,,	481
Unpresented cheques	117
Loan interest paid to bank, not entered in cash book	70
Amounts paid into bank, but not credited by bank until 3.4.19. .	147

25

9 From the cash book and bank statement given below prepare a bank reconciliation statement as at 31st January, 19...

CASH BOOK

			£					£
January	1	Balance	1 000	January	1	H. & C. Ltd	001	150
,,	3	Sales	200	,,	4	Wages	002	100
,,	7	B. Brown	100	,,	6	H.M. & Co.	003	50
,,	11	Sales	300	,,	10	Equipment Ltd	004	200
,,	16	G. Gray	150	,,	14	Wages	005	50
,,	21	Sales	400	,,	18	H.M. & Co.	006	125
,,	27	-do-	200	,,	22	Wages	007	100
,,	31	W. Green	150	,,	29	Catering Co.	008	25
				,,	31	H. & C. Ltd	009	100

BANK STATEMENT

Date			Debit	Credit	Balance
			£	£	£
January	1	Balance			1 000
,,	3	001	150		850
,,	4	Cash		200	1 050
,,	5	002	100		950
,,	8	Cash		100	1 050
,,	10	003	50		1 000
,,	12	Cash		300	1 300
,,	15	005	50		1 250
,,	17	Cash		150	1 400
,,	20	006	125		1 275
,,	22	Cash		400	1 675
,,	23	007	100		1 575
,,	28	Cash		200	1 775
,,	31	Chgs.	5		1 770

CHAPTER 3

Accounting for purchases

From the accounting point of view the purchases of a business fall into two categories: cash purchases and credit purchases. When food, drink, etc., are purchased, for cash, there is an immediate exchange of cash for the commodities purchased: all that need be recorded in the books of the business is, therefore, the payment of the purchase price and the acquisition of the goods purchased.

When food, drink, etc., are purchased on credit, the business acquires the commodities concerned but the settlement of the purchase price (i.e. payment of the amount due) is delayed until several weeks (or sometimes months) later. In the meantime a debt exists from the business to the supplier of the goods (creditor) and this must be reflected in the supplier's account in the ledger.

Cash purchases

The treatment of cash purchases is simple. All payments made in respect of food, drink, tobaccos, etc., purchased for cash are credited in the cash book and debited in the purchases account. For example, if a hotel buys provisions worth £50 for cash, the double entry will be made as shown in Figure 25.

Cash Book

					19.. Apr	23	Purchases	50	00

Purchases A/c

19.. Apr	23	Cash	50	00					

Figure 25

It will be observed that no entry is made in the personal account of the supplier. The transaction is fully settled and, thus, the identity of the supplier is of no consequence.

Credit purchases

When goods are purchased on credit, the payment of the amount due to the supplier does not take place until some time after the delivery of such goods. In the meantime, the supplier of the goods is a creditor to the business in that money is owing to him in respect of the goods with which he has parted. The debt due to the supplier is represented by a credit entry in his personal account. Double entry in respect of credit purchases is given in Figure 26.

Provision Suppliers Ltd

					19.. Apr	23	Purchases	50	00

Purchases A/c

19.. Apr	23	Provision Sup. Ltd	50	00					

Figure 26

Whenever goods are purchased on credit the buyer receives, either together with the goods or a few days later, an *invoice*. This shows particulars of the goods, such as the quantity, price per unit, description, and the total amount due.

Hotel and catering establishments which are sufficiently large in size purchase from wholesalers rather than retailers. In such circumstances a *trade discount* is often allowed by the supplier. This is a deduction from the amount due and would only be extended to establishments buying sufficiently large quantities. Trade discount is *not* recorded in the books: all goods purchased are entered net, after deduction of trade discount.

A specimen invoice is given in Figure 27.

HOTEL AND CATERING SUPPLIERS LTD.,
5, WEST END LANE, LONDON, W.16.

TO: *Imperial Hotel Ltd.*
Leicester Square
London, W.1.

INVOICE No: 7361
16th June 1971

	Size	Quantity	Price Per Unit	£	p
X.L. Café Blend Coffee	½ kg	20 kg	£0.70	28	00
Olive Oil	5L	50L	£2.00	20	00
S.M.F. Beans	1 Kg	10 Kg	£1.00	10	00
				58	00
Less Trade Discount –	10%			5	80
			Net Due	52	20

Figure 27

As already mentioned, double entry in respect of credit purchases is completed by debiting the purchases account and crediting the account of the supplier. It will be appreciated, however, that the number of invoices received is usually very large; many hotel and catering establishments receive hundreds of invoices each month. It would, therefore, be inconvenient to debit each separate invoice in the purchases account and, also, unusual to show this amount of detail in the ledger.

Consequently, purchase invoices are recorded as follows:

(1) All invoices, having been numbered consecutively, are entered individually in a subsidiary book known as the *purchases day book*, and
(2) Double entry is completed by:
(a) crediting the invoices in the accounts of suppliers individually;
(b) debiting the periodical (weekly, monthly) total of the purchases day book in the purchases account.

In this way the number of debit entries in the purchases account is reduced considerably. As double entry is completed in the ledger, the entering of invoices in the purchases day book does not count for double entry purposes.

Example The following invoices are received by the Kensington Restaurant:

January	1	B. Baker & Sons	£55
,,	3	A. G. Grocer & Co.	25
,,	5	H. & C. Suppliers Ltd	20
,,	8	B. Baker & Sons	45
,,	11	A. G. Grocer & Co.	35
,,	14	Food Sellers Ltd	5
,,	17	H. & C. Suppliers Ltd	10
,,	20	B. Baker & Sons	15
,,	24	H. & C. Suppliers Ltd	50
,,	27	Food Sellers Ltd	30
,,	29	A. G. Grocer & Co.	20
,,	31	Food Sellers Ltd	25

The invoices are entered in the purchases day book (Figure 28) of the restaurant and posted to appropriate accounts in the ledger (Figure 29).

When posting, the folio number of the purchases day book is entered in the account concerned and the folio number of the purchases account is entered in the purchases day book.

				Inv. No.	Led. Fol.		
		Purchases Day Book					27
DATE							
19..					L		
Jan.	1	B. Baker a Sons.		1	51	55	00
"	3	A.G. Grocer a Co.		2	L 53	25	00
"	5	H a C Suppliers Ltd.		3	L 55	20	00
"	8	B. Baker a Sons.		4	L 51	45	00
"	11	A.G Grocer a Co.		5	L 53	35	00
"	14	Food Sellers Ltd.		6	L 57	5	00
"	17	H a C Suppliers Ltd.		7	L 55	10	00
"	20	B. Baker a Sons.		8	L 51	15	00
"	24	H a C Suppliers Ltd.		9	L 55	50	00
"	27	Food Sellers Ltd.		10	L 57	30	00
"	29	A.G. Grocer a Co.		11	L 53	20	00
"	31	Food Sellers Ltd.		12	L 57	25	00
"	31	Transferred to Purchases A/c			L 106	335	00

Figure 28

				B. Baker a Sons			51
				19..			
				Jan 1 Purchases	PB 27	55	00
				" 8 — do —	PB 27	45	00
				" 20 — do —	PB 27	15	00
				A.G. Grocer a Co.			53
				19..			
				Jan 3 Purchases	PB 27	25	00
				" 11 — do —	PB 27	35	00
				" 29 — do —	PB 27	20	00

Figure 29 (a)

				H & C Suppliers Ltd.				55	
				19..					
				Jan	5	Purchases	PB 27	20	00
				"	17	— do —	PB 27	10	00
				"	24	— do —	PB 27	50	00
				Food Sellers Ltd				57	
				19..					
				Jan	14	Purchases	PB 27	5	00
				"	27	— do —	PB 27	30	00
				"	31	— do —	PB 27	25	00
				Purchases A/c				106	
19..									
Jan	31	Sundries	PB 27	335	00				

Figure 29 (b)

Purchases returns Sometimes goods which have previously been purchased have to be returned to the seller. This may be necessary when they are found to be defective in quality or damaged. Again, sometimes the seller over-charges for the goods. As a result, it often becomes necessary for a supplier to reduce the amount charged on an invoice already sent to a customer. This is done by means of a *credit note*.

A specimen credit note is shown in Figure 30.

HOTEL AND CATERING SUPPLIERS LTD.
5, West End Lane, London, W. 16.

TO: *Imperial Hotel Ltd.*
Leicester Square
London, W. 1.

CREDIT NOTE
26ᵀᴴ *December 1971*

	£.	P
By Overcharge per invoice dated 1·9·1941		
Amount Charged — £20·00		
Less Correct Charge - 15·00	5	00

Figure 30

Note: It is assumed that the invoice dated 1st Sept. 1971, was not subject to a trade discount. Otherwise the percentage of trade discount would have to be deducted from the amount of the above credit note.

The accounting treatment of a credit note is as follows:

(1) All credit notes, having been numbered consecutively, are entered individually in a subsidiary book, called the *purchases returns book*.
(2) Double entry is completed by:
(a) debiting the credit notes in the accounts of suppliers individually;
(b) crediting the periodical (weekly, monthly) total of the purchases returns account in the ledger.

At the end of the accounting period the balance of the purchases returns account is transferred to the purchases account. The latter will thus show the net purchases for the year.

Example   A hotel receives the following credit notes during the month of January, 19..:

January	6	Brompton Food Market Ltd	£6
,,	13	X.Y.Z. Wines Co.	10
,,	25	Brompton Food Market Ltd	2
,,	31	B.S.L. Grocers	5

The above credit notes are entered in the purchases returns book of the hotel (Figure 31) and posted to appropriate ledger accounts (Figure 32).

Figure 31

19..							Brompton Food Market Ltd.			77	
Jan	6	Returns	PR 32	6	00						
,,	25	— do —	PR 32	2	00						
							X. Y. Z. Wines Co.			79	
19..											
Jan	13	Returns	PR 32	10	00						
							B. S. L. Grocers			81	
19..											
Jan	31	Returns	PR 32	5	00						
							Purchases Returns A/c			109	
						19..					
						Jan	31	Sundries	PR 32	23	00

Figure 32

Statement of account

Most suppliers who sell goods on credit send their customers a statement of account (usually monthly). This is a copy of the buyer's account in the books of the supplier and shows particulars of invoices and any credit notes sent to the customer, any cash received and, of course, the balance due to the supplier at the end of the period.

It is usual to check all suppliers' statements against their accounts in the ledger. Any cash discount offered should then be deducted before payment is made. The treatment of cash discounts was explained in Chapter 2. A specimen statement of account is shown in Figure 33, on the next page.

Assuming that this statement is paid within one month (i.e. before the end of July), a cash discount of £2.75 would be deducted from the amount due and a cheque for £52.25 drawn in favour of the supplier.

HOTEL AND CATERING SUPPLIERS LTD.
5. WEST END LANE. LONDON W 16

TO: *Imperial Hotel Ltd.,*
Leicester Square,
London, W. 1.

STATEMENT

30th. June, 1971

Terms: 5% monthly

DATE		£	P
June 1	Goods	20	00
„ 6	„	12	00
„ 16	„	18	00
„ 28	„	10	00
		60	00
„ 12	Returns	5	00
	Balance Due	55	00

Figure 33

Example The following transactions took place between a hotel and Hotel Supplies Co.:

January 1	Goods purchased		£20
„ 4	„ „		15
„ 13	„ „		20
„ 21	„ „		25
„ 27	„ returned		5
„ 31	„ purchased		25
February 2	„ „		20
„ 10	Cash paid to supplier		95
„ 10	Discount received from supplier		5

The account of Hotel Supplies Co. is written up in the ledger of the hotel; and the account balanced as at the end of January. See Figure 34.

Hotel Supplies Co.

19..					19..				
Jan	27	Returns		5 00	Jan	1	Purchases		20 00
"	31	Balance	c/d	100 00	"	4	— do —		15 00
					"	13	— do —		20 00
					"	21	— do —		25 00
					"	31	— do —		25 00
				105 00					105 00
19..					19..				
Feb	10	Cash		95 00	Feb.	1	Balance	b/d	100 00
"	10	Disc. Received		5 00	"	2	Purchases		20 00

Figure 34

Problems   **1** Distinguish clearly between cash discount and trade discount.

2 Write short notes on the purpose of invoice; credit note; and statement of account.

3 On 1st December, 19.., after eleven months' trading, Jack Mason had the following balances in his books:

Capital	£2 200
Sales	1 750
Purchases	620
Cash at Bank	840
Premises	1 725
Wages	370
China and Cutlery	80
Furniture	125
Insurance	15
Kitchen Equipment	250
Gas and Electricity	75
Creditors: V. A. Rigby	50
O. Kay	100

(continued)

Arrange these in the form of a trial balance and enter balances in accounts. Mason's transactions in December were:

December	2	Purchased provisions by cheque	£150
,,	6	Paid for kitchen equipment by cheque	50
,,	10	Paid amount due to O. Kay	100
,,	14	Banked sales to date	85
,,	16	Paid wages by cheque	60
,,	19	Paid rates by cheque	77
,,	23	Bought groceries on credit: V. A. Rigby	120
		A. M. Williams	60
,,	27	Paid by cheque for insurance to 31st March, 19..	15
,,	31	Banked sales to date	141

Enter these transactions in Mason's books and extract a trial balance as at 31st December, 19...

4 On 1st January, 19.., John Brown started in business with a capital in cash of £5 000. In January, his transactions were:

January	1	Paid by cheque rent for premises	£1 100
,,	2	Paid by cheque for furniture	200
,,	4	Paid by cheque for kitchen equipment	400
,,	6	Paid wages by cheque	65
,,	8	Credit purchases: F. W. Young & Co.	33
		V. Fatt & Son	22
		Jack Player & Son	16
,,	10	Banked cash sales	57
,,	14	Paid by cheque for provisions	36
,,	19	Paid wages by cheque	66
,,	22	Credit purchases: Jack Player & Son	13
		V. Fatt & Son	27
		F. W. Young & Co.	46
,,	23	Paid by cheque for stationery	12
,,	25	Credit purchases: F. W. Young & Co.	26
		Five Squares Ltd	15
		V. Fatt & Son	19
,,	26	Banked cash sales	219
,,	28	Paid wages by cheque	72
,,	29	Paid for advertising by cheque	50
,,	30	Received credit notes from: V. Fatt & Son	5
		F. W. Young & Co.	3
		Jack Player & Son	4
,,	31	Banked cash sales	116
,,	31	Paid by cheque for groceries	33

Enter the above transactions in appropriate books, post to ledger, and extract Brown's trial balance as at 31st January, 19...

5 Jack Lane commenced business on 1st January, 19.., as a café proprietor with £2 000 in the bank.

His transactions in January were as follows:

January	1	Purchased leasehold premises, paid by cheque	£1 350
,,	2	Purchased furniture, paid by cheque	50
,,	3	Withdrew for petty cash	20
,,	3	Paid by cheque for fruit and vegetables	37
,,	4	Received invoices from:	
		A. N. B. Grocers Ltd	35
		O. K. Provisions Ltd	42
		B. S. Fish & Sons	16
,,	7	Paid wages by cheque	39
,,	8	Paid by cheque for kitchen equipment	210
,,	9	Paid out of petty cash:	
		Stationery	3
		Postage	2
		Cleaning materials	2
,,	10	Banked sales	125
,,	11	Invoices received from:	
		O. K. Provisions Ltd	12
		B. S. Fish & Sons	19
		Battersea Fruiterers	18
,,	14	Banked sales	136
,,	15	Paid wages by cheque	46
,,	17	Paid by cheque for groceries	21
,,	19	Invoices received from:	
		A. N. B. Grocers Ltd	26
		Battersea Fruiterers	13
		B. S. Fish & Sons	22
,,	21	Banked sales	176
,,	23	Paid out of petty cash:	
		Cleaning materials	3
		Postage	3
		Travelling expenses	1
,,	24	Credit notes received from:	
		O. K. Provisions Ltd	3
		A. N. B. Grocers Ltd	4
,,	25	Paid wages by cheque	47
,,	27	Banked sales	42
,,	28	Paid by cheque for electricity	86
,,	29	Petty cash payments:	
		Stationery	2
		Travelling expenses	1
,,	30	Credit notes received from:	
		Battersea Fruiterers	5
		B. S. Fish & Sons	4
,,	31	Paid wages by cheque	39

You are required to write up Lane's books in respect of the month of January, 19.., and extract his trial balance as at the end of that period.

CHAPTER 4

Accounting for sales

Cash sales The sales of a business may be of two kinds: cash sales and credit sales. A cash sale takes place when food, drink, etc., are sold and the price is paid immediately. As soon as the price is paid by the customer, the transaction is fully settled. From the book-keeping point of view all that is needed is an entry in the cash book (to show that cash has been received) and an entry in the sales account (to show that something has been sold).

Hence, the double entry in respect of cash sales is:

Dr.   cash book
Cr.   sales account

Example On 1st April, 19.., the cash sales of a restaurant amounted to £425, and were paid into the bank the same day. This is recorded in the books of the restaurant (Figure 35).

				L							12
19..			*Cash Book*								
Apr	1	Sales		47	425	00					

			Sales A/c							47
						19-..		CB		
						Apr	1	Cash	12	425	00

Figure 35

Credit sales The treatment of credit sales is different and may vary from one type of hotel and catering establishment to another. Within a particular business, e.g. a hotel, there may be several distinct methods of recording credit sales. In general, however, credit sales in hotels and catering establishments fall into three main categories.

First, there are *restaurant sales*. These include all food, drinks, etc., sold on credit to non-residents, paying their accounts periodically (usually monthly). Next there are *banqueting sales*: these include all the banqueting sales in respect of which there is no immediate settlement. Finally, there are short-term credit sales to the guests of a hotel recorded in the *tabular* or *visitors' ledger*.

Restaurant sales The general method of recording the credit sales of a restaurant is the same whether these are sales to non-residents dining in a hotel or expense-account customers dining in a restaurant. Briefly, the procedure may be described as follows.

When the customer has been served, the waiter prepares a bill, usually in duplicate. This is signed by the customer, who takes the top copy of the bill, Figure 36.

No. 116

BLUEBELL RESTAURANT
16, Second Avenue
London, W.1.

Table No. *9*   Date *16ᵗʰ May, 1971*

Waiter No. *12*   No. of Covers *2*

	£	p
2 × Crème de Champignons		20
Mixed Grill		60
Escalope de Veau		70
2 × Pommes Santées		15
2 × Haricots Verts		30
2 × Fruit Salad		40
TOTAL MEALS	2	35
1 Bot. Nuits St. Georges	1	20
1 Tia Maria		20
TOTAL WINES, SPIRITS	1	40
TOTAL	3	75

Figure 36

The second (carbon) copy of the bill is sent to the accounts department. Here, all such bills in respect of credit sales are numbered consecutively and entered in a subsidiary book, the *restaurant sales book.*

Double entry is completed by debiting each individual bill in a customer's personal account, and crediting the periodical (weekly or monthly) total of such sales in the sales account in the ledger.

Example   The following are the credit sales of the Bluebell Restaurant:

January	1	Midland Motors Ltd	£3
,,	2	Business Promotions Ltd	4
,,	3	B. M. Blake, Esq.	5
,,	4	Midland Motors Ltd	12
,,	4	Business Promotions Ltd	6
,,	5	B. M. Blake, Esq.	2
,,	6	Midland Motors Ltd	8
,,	7	Business Promotions Ltd	10

The above transactions are entered in the restaurant sales book (Figure 37) and posted to ledger accounts, Figure 38.

BOOK-KEEPING IN THE HOTEL AND CATERING INDUSTRY

Restaurant Sales Book				Bill No.	Led. Fol.			36	
DATE									
19.. Jan.		1	Midland Motors Ltd.	1	L/101			3	00
..		2	Business Promotions Ltd.	2	L/103			4	00
..		3	B.M. Blake, Esq.	3	L/104			5	00
..		4	Midland Motors Ltd.	4	L/101			12	00
..		4	Business Promotions Ltd.	5	L/103			6	00
..		5	B.M. Blake, Esq.	6	L/104			2	00
..		6	Midland Motors Ltd.	7	L/101			8	00
..		7	Business Promotions Ltd.	8	L/103			10	00
..		7	Transferred to Sales A/c		L/201			50	00

Figure 37 (above)

Figure 38 (below)

			Midland Motors Ltd.					101	
19.. Jan	1	Sales	SB 36	3	00				
..	4	— do —	SB 36	12	00				
..	6	— do —	SB 36	8	00				

			Business Promotions Ltd					103	
19.. Jan	2	Sales	SB 36	4	00				
..	4	— do —	SB 36	6	00				
..	7	— do —	SB 36	10	00				

			B.M. Blake Esq.					104	
19.. Jan	3	Sales	SB 36	5	00				
..	5	— do —	SB 36	2	00				

			Sales A/c						
				19.. Jan	7	Sundries	SB 36	50	00

On receipt of the amount due from a customer, the cash book is debited and the account of the customer is credited. Thus, if Midland Motors paid the amount due on 31st January, 19.., their account would appear as in Figure 39.

19..					19..					
Jan	1	Sales	SB 36	3 00	Jan	31	Cash	CB	23 00	
"	4	– do –	SB 36	12 00						
"	6	– do –	SB 36	8 00						
				23 00					23 00	

Figure 39

Banqueting sales

From the point of view of the book-keeping involved, the treatment of banqueting sales proper is similar to that of the various functions such as wedding receptions, dinner parties, conferences, etc. We will, therefore, refer to all such sales as banqueting sales.

The arrangements with the client organizing the banquet may vary quite considerably. The organizer may agree to pay so much per cover for the meals only, in which event all drinks ordered by those taking part in the banquet would have to be paid for in cash. Any such drinks would be treated as bar cash sales.

Another common arrangement is for the organizer to agree to pay a given charge per cover for the meals and, additionally, request that a given number of bottles of wine be made available to members of the party. Then, both the meals and the wines are sold on credit.

Whatever the arrangements made, it is clear that a distinction should be made between what the organizer has agreed to pay for (credit sales) and any additional drinks, cigars, and cigarettes required by particular members of the party and supplied on a cash basis.

The nature of the book-keeping records kept in respect of banqueting sales depends on the volume of banqueting business done and on the frequency of banquets undertaken for particular clients.

Where the volume of banqueting is small, it is sometimes the practice to treat all banqueting sales as if they were cash sales. No entries would then be made until such time as the client settled his account. The cash book would then be debited and the sales account credited with the amount received.

It must be pointed out that this procedure is not in accordance with the best accounting practice, as the books of the business do not reflect the true financial state of affairs.

Where the volume of banqueting business is substantial, it is usual to open a separate *banqueting sales book*. Particulars of banqueting credit sales are recorded in the same manner as are restaurant credit sales in the restaurant sales book (see p. 46).

Clients making frequent use of the banqueting facilities of the hotel/restaurant would have a proper ledger account opened for them. All such accounts would be posted in the same way as those illustrated on p.46. Clients using the banqueting facilities infrequently (e.g. wedding receptions, twenty-first dinner parties, association annual dinners) may have a composite account opened for them, Figure 40.

41

Figure 40 Banqueting debtors' account

Whenever a banqueting debtor settles his/her account, a debit entry is made in the cash book and a corresponding credit entry in the banqueting debtors account. The total amount of outstanding debts may easily be determined by reference to the banqueting debtors account. In the above specimen account this amounts to £120.

ROOM	1	2	3	4	5	6	7	8	9	10	DAILY SUMMARY	
NAME	Fenton	Black	James	Stein	Dewey	Saxton	Turner	Weston	Bentley			
No of VISITORS	1	1	2	2	1	2	2	1	1			
Balance b/f	3 50	6 70	7 60	1 95	2 30	8 90	9 80	14 30			Balance b/f	55 05
Apartments	1 50	1 50	2 50	2 50	1 50	2 50			1 50		Apartments	13 50
Breakfasts	25	25	50	50	25	50	50	25			Breakfasts	3 00
E.M. Teas	10			20	10						E.M. Teas	40
Luncheons		60	1 55	1 70	75	1 80			70		Luncheons	7 10
Afternoon Teas	15		30		15	30			15		Afternoon Teas	1 05
Dinners	85	95		2 10		2 25			85		Dinners	7 00
Liquors		60		80		1 20			20		Liquors	2 80
Telephone	05		50		05						Telephone	60
Miscellaneous	40				50				1 25		Miscellaneous	2 15
Paid Out		15		40		1 80					Paid Out	2 35
Total	6 80	10 75	12 95	10 15	5 60	19 25	10 30	14 55	4 65		Total	95 00
Cash								14 55			Cash	14 55
Ledger							10·30				Ledger	10 30
Allowances					50						Allowances	50
Balance c/f	6 80	10 75	12 95	10 15	5 10	19 25			4 65		Balance c/f	69 65
Total	6 80	10 75	12 95	10 15	5 60	19 25	10 30	14 55	4 65		Total	95 00

Figure 41 Hotel visitors' ledger (vertical type)

Hotel visitors'   The most convenient way of keeping the accounts of hotel guests is to maintain a
ledger   hotel visitors' ledger, also known as the tabular ledger.

Of all the accounting records kept by hotels this is certainly the one in most common use and, therefore, deserves a more detailed description. Because of its layout, many students find difficulty in understanding how it is compiled and how it fits into the general scheme of double entry. These two aspects of the hotel visitors' ledger will, therefore, be dealt with first.

Layout   The specimen visitors' ledger shown in Figure 41 may be divided horizontally into two sections: the upper section, including the totals, and the lower section, including the second line of totals.

The upper section contains the debit side of visitors' accounts, and is used to record the balances owing from visitors, brought forward from the previous day, and the charges made to visitors during the day concerned.

The lower section contains the credit side of visitors' accounts and is used to record any cash paid by visitors in settling their accounts; any transfers from the visitors' ledger to a personal account in the sales ledger; allowances, if any, made to visitors; and the balances owing from visitors at the end of the current day carried forward to the following day.

Vertically, the visitors' ledger may also be divided into two sections: the personal accounts of visitors on the left-hand side and the somewhat smaller 'daily summary section' on the right-hand side. The latter shows the daily totals of entries made in the individual accounts of the guests.

Double entry   Although different from a conventional ledger, the visitors' ledger is a proper ledger, consisting of the personal accounts of the visitors. In fact, each of the visitors' accounts could be re-written and presented as a conventional, double-sided account. Thus, Fenton's account could be re-written as in Figure 42.

Dr						Fenton – Room 1				Cr
19..						19..				
May	3	Balance	b/d	3	50	May 3 Balance	c/d	6	80	
"	3	Sales		1	50					
"	3	– do –			25					
"	3	– do –			10					
"	3	– do –			15					
"	3	– do –			85					
"	3	– do –			05					
"	3	– do –			40					
				6	80			6	80	
19..										
May	4	Balance	b/d	6	80					

Figure 42

Charges debited to visitors are totalled in the last column of the visitors' ledger and, daily, transferred to the monthly summary sheet. This is totalled monthly and the individual totals posted to the appropriate accounts in the ledger. A specimen monthly summary sheet is given in Figure 43.

MONTHLY SUMMARY SHEET   May. 19..

DATE	APART-MENTS	B/FASTS	E.M. TEAS	LUNCHES	A/NOON TEAS	DINNERS	LIQUORS	TELEPHONE	MISCEL-LANEOUS	DAILY TOTAL	ALLOW-ANCES
May 1	15 00	3 25	60	11 30	2 10	9 60	4 95	1 65	95	49 40	75
" 2	13 00	3 50	35	8 60	1 70	8 10	3 15	30	1 60	40 30	
" 3	13 50	3 00	40	7 10	1 05	7 00	2 80	60	2 15	37 60	50
etc.											
" 31											
TOTAL	440 00	80 00	20 00	300 00	40 00	380 00	150 00	45 00	60 00	1515 00	10 00

Figure 43 Monthly summary sheet

Note: (1) Column headings in the monthly summary sheet correspond with the sequence of charges in the hotel visitors' ledger. (2) No column is provided for the paid outs because (a) monthly summary sheet is a summary of sales, (b) double entry in respect of paid outs is completed by crediting the petty cash book and debiting visitors' accounts in the visitors' ledger.

Assuming that by the end of May the total of apartments sales is £440, this would be posted in the ledger (Figure 44).

Sales A/c - Apartments

								19..					
								Jan	31	M.S.S.		290	00
								Feb	28	—do—		340	00
								Mar	31	—do—		415	00
								Apr	30	—do—		430	00
								May	31	—do—		440	00

Figure 44 Sales account—apartments

To sum up, double entry in respect of sales (charges) to visitors is completed by debiting the individual charges in the visitors' accounts in the visitors' ledger, and crediting the monthly totals from the monthly summary sheet in the appropriate accounts in the ledger.

Any allowances made to guests should be properly authorized by the management. As may be seen from the specimen visitors' ledger, these are credited in visitors' accounts (see Dewey, Room 5), entered in the allowances column of the monthly summary sheet and, at the end of each month, debited in the allowances account in the ledger.

The treatment of cash received from visitors is simple: the cash book is debited and the account of the visitor credited (see Weston, Room 8).

Sometimes a guest leaves the hotel without, for one reason or another, paying his account. When that happens there is, clearly, no point in keeping the guest's account in the visitors' ledger. The balance owing on the guest's departure is, therefore, transferred from the visitors' ledger to a personal account in the sales ledger.

In the specimen visitors' ledger given above, Turner left the hotel on 3rd May, 19.., without settling his account. Consequently, his account in the visitors' ledger is credited with £10.30. The corresponding debit entry in his account in the sales ledger would appear as is shown in Figure 45.

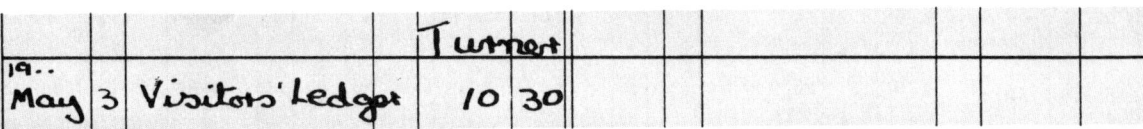

		Turner							
19.. May	3	Visitors' Ledger	10	30					

Figure 45 Turner's account

Assuming that a few weeks later Turner sends the hotel a cheque for £10.30 in settlement, this would be debited in the cash book and credited in his account, thus balancing the latter.

The monthly summary sheet (Figure 43) is fairly typical of those in actual use in hotels. It has, however, one serious deficiency: the allowances to customers are not analysed and, as a result, at the end of each month it is impossible to post figures of *net sales* to the ledger. *Gross sales* are posted to the credit of the various ledger accounts, and the total of monthly allowances to the debit of allowances account. In consequence, at the end of a trading period, it is impossible under this method to ascertain the exact amount of profit from any one department.

In order to remedy this, it is possible to maintain a monthly allowances sheet in conjunction with the monthly summary sheet. Under this method, allowances to visitors are analysed daily and totalled at the end of each month. They are then deducted from the gross sales in the monthly summary sheet. The resulting net sales are then posted to the ledger.

A specimen monthly allowances sheet is given in Figure 46.

MONTHLY ALLOWANCES SHEET   May 19..

Date	Apartment		Break-fasts		E.M.Teas		Luncheons		A/Noon Tea		Dinners		Liquors		Telephone		Misc.		Total	
May 1											40		35						75	
" 3							25										25		50	
etc. Monthly Total	2	00	1	00	1	50		50		50	2	00	1	50		50		50	10	00

Figure 46 Monthly allowances sheet

The monthly summary sheet shown in Figure 47 is a variant of the conventional type. Its main advantage is that it shows a figure of net sales for each section of the turnover.

It will be appreciated that when this type of monthly summary sheet is used there is no necessity for an allowances account in the ledger.

MONTHLY SUMMARY SHEET												May, 19..
Date	Apartments	B/fasts	E.M.Teas	Lunches	A/Noon Teas	Dinners	Liquors	Telephone	Miscellaneous	Daily Total	Less Allowances	Net Total
May 1	15 00	3 25	60	11 30	2 10	9 60	4 95	1 65	95	49 40	75	48 65
" 2	13 00	3 50	35	8 60	1 70	8 10	3 15	30	1 60	40 30		40 30
" 3	13 50	3 00	40	7 10	1 05	7 00	2 80	60	2 15	37 60	50	37 10
etc.												
Monthly Total	440 00	80 00	20 00	300 00	40 00	380 00	150 00	45 00	60 00	1515 00	10 00	1505 00
Less Allowances	2 00	1 00	1 50	50	50	2 00	1 50	50	50	10 00		
NET TOTAL	438 00	79 00	18 50	299 50	39 50	378 00	148 50	44 50	59 50	1505 00		

Figure 47

Sources of charges   The charges incurred by visitors may be numerous and arise in various parts of the hotel. The purpose of the present section is to explain where they originate and how they find their way to the visitors' accounts.

Apartments   This basic charge is incurred by all guests who stay at least one night. The charge originates in the reception office and is determined by reference to the room list or room index or the terms book. The charge is debited to the visitor's account as soon as such an account is opened. On subsequent days the charge is usually debited to the visitor each evening for the coming night's stay. In the specimen visitors' ledger on p. 42, Turner (Room 7) and Weston (Room 8) left the hotel after breakfast. No charge for apartments is, therefore, debited to them. Bentley (Room 9) arrives before luncheon and is debited £1.50 in respect of the coming night's stay (3rd/4th May).

Meals   This heading, for the purpose of the visitors' ledger, includes all meals and non-alcoholic drinks, such as teas and coffees. In respect of each such meal it is usual to raise a duplicate voucher (Figure 48), a copy of which is passed to the book-keeper for debiting a visitor's account. It is important, particularly in the case of transient hotels, that this is done as soon as possible. Otherwise a guest may leave the hotel before certain charges are debited. The second copy of such a voucher is usually passed on to the control office for checking purposes.

Figure 48 Duplicate voucher

Drinks   This heading includes all alcoholic beverages and, usually, minerals. A charge in respect of drinks may originate in a dispense bar, a cocktail bar, or the lounge. The procedure adopted is the same as in the case of meals. It is usual for the person dispensing the drinks to price the voucher, though in some hotels this may be left to the book-keeper responsible for the visitors' ledger.

Sundry sales   In addition to the three basic charges—apartments, meals, and drinks—there are numerous other charges (e.g. telephone, laundry, valeting, garage, etc.) that may be incurred by a visitor. Here again, the general rule is that a voucher in duplicate must be made out and a copy thereof sent to the book-keeper for debiting the visitor's account.

Visitors' paid outs   This heading includes various amounts paid out by the employees of the hotel on behalf of visitors. Examples of such paid outs are theatre tickets, flowers, and payments for C.O.D. mail addressed to the visitors. Any such payments would be credited to the petty cash book. A duplicate voucher would then be made out and a copy of it passed to the book-keeper responsible for visitors' accounts.

It is important that a distinction be drawn between visitors' paid outs and sundry sales. The former is a recovery of the hotel's payments and is not a part of current revenue; the latter is, of course, as much a part of the hotel's revenue as meals, drinks, and other similar charges. It will be appreciated that what is a visitors' paid out (V.P.O.) in one hotel may well be regarded as a sundry sale in another. Thus where visitors' laundry is sent out, any charges made to them would normally be regarded as V.P.O. Where a hotel has a laundry of its own, any charges made to visitors would contain an element of profit and would, therefore, be regarded as sundry sales.

Guests' bills   In addition to opening an account in the visitors' ledger, the book-keeper will open a bill for each guest on his/her arrival. Guests' bills are written up daily from the duplicate vouchers which are debited in the visitors' ledger.

It will be appreciated that, as identical charges are entered in the visitors' ledger and in the guests' bills, when all vouchers have been posted all balances in the visitors' ledger will correspond with the balances shown by guests' bills. In fact, as soon as all charges have been posted it is usual to compare the two sets of balances. Any differences should be investigated and put right before carrying the balances to the following day. A specimen guest's bill is shown in Figure 49.

GRAND HOTEL LTD. To: M.A. James, Esq. Room: 126	2nd May		3rd May		4th May			
Balance b/f			7	60	12	95		
Apartments	2	50	2	50				
Breakfasts				50		50		
E.M. Teas								
Luncheons	3	75	1	55				
A/Noon Teas		35		30				
Dinners								
Liquors		65						
Telephone				50				
Miscellaneous								
Paid Out		35						
Balance c/f	7	60	12	95	13	45		
Deposits/Allowances					–	–		
Amount Due					13	45		

Figure 49 A specimen bill

There are two main kinds of guests' bills: four-day bills (as illustrated above) and eight-day bills. The choice of the kind of bill used depends on the average length of stay of the guests. Thus transient and other short-stay hotels tend to use four-day bills, whereas resort hotels tend to use eight-day bills. There is, of course, no reason why a hotel should not use both kinds.

Treatment of deposits

It is customary in many hotels to require deposits in respect of any advance bookings made by guests. Even where that is not so, some customers will send a deposit to ensure that a room is properly booked for them.

It must be realized that advance deposits do not represent current revenue (sales) but must be regarded as amounts owing to guests. It is not until such time as the guest arrives and incurs charges in excess of the deposit that the latter may be treated as current revenue.

There are several different methods of recording such deposits in the books of a hotel. The two most popular methods are outlined below.

Under the first method the deposit received is debited in the cash book and credited in a personal account opened for the intending visitor in the sales ledger. On the visitor's departure, the balance from his personal account (i.e. the deposit) must be transferred to the credit side of his account in the visitors' ledger.

Under the second method, the treatment of advance deposits is the same except that a separate account is not opened for each deposit. Instead a composite account is opened for all deposits received. This is illustrated in Figure 50.

The credit balance of the advance deposits account represents the total amount of deposits received but not yet transferred to the visitors' ledger. Any deposits returned to guests, for one reason or another, would be credited in the hotel's cash book and debited in the advance deposits account.

En pension terms

Many hotels, particularly resort hotels, offer *en pension* terms or terms inclusive of certain specified meals. There are two main methods of dealing with *en pension* terms in the visitors' ledger.

Date		Room No.	£	p	Date		Date of Arrival	£	p
19..					19..				
May 28	Visitors Ledger	116	10	00	Jan 29	Mr & Mrs Goode	May 21	10	00
					Feb 22	V. Browne	July 2	5	00
June 20	— do —	347	5	00	Mar 16	H. George	June 16	5	00
July 5	— do —	118	10	00	„ 25	Mr & Mrs Fisher	June 29	10	00
					Apr 3	Mr & Mrs Henry	Aug 11	10	00

Advance Deposits A/c

Figure 50 Advance deposits account

Under the first method, the procedure is as follows:

(1) The weekly inclusive charge is divided by seven to arrive at the daily charge.

(2) The daily charge is debited in the visitors' ledger in an *en pension* column (line). This additional column is usually placed between the 'balances b/f' column and the 'apartments' column.

From the visitors' ledger the daily total of the inclusive charges would be transferred to an *en pension* column of the monthly summary sheet, in the same manner as all other charges to visitors. Similarly, at the end of each month the total of inclusive charges in the monthly summary sheet would be posted to the credit of the *en pension* account in the ledger.

Under the second method, the procedure is as follows:

(1) The weekly inclusive charge is divided by seven to arrive at the daily charge.

(2) The daily charge is divided into a number of component parts (e.g. apartments, breakfast, luncheon, dinner) according to what is included in the terms.

(3) Each separate component part of the inclusive charge is debited in the visitors' ledger in the usual manner.

Example The *en pension* terms of a hotel are £15.75 per week. On the basis of past experience the apportionment is: food—$66\frac{2}{3}$ per cent; apartments—$33\frac{1}{3}$ per cent Following the second method above:

$$\text{the daily charge is } \frac{£15.75}{7} = £2.25$$

Of the daily charge:

the charge for apartments = £0.75
„   „   „ food   = £1.50

Assuming that the *en pension* terms include breakfast, lunch and dinner, the £1.50 charged for food might then be apportioned as follows:

Breakfast	25p
Lunch	55p
Dinner	70p
Total	£1.50

This second method is preferable to the first as, due to the analysis of the inclusive charge, all sales to visitors are recorded in a uniform manner. On the other hand, it is clear that the analysis of the inclusive charge is to an extent a matter of judgement, as there is no precise method of determining how much of the total should be credited to food and how much to apartments. It may be added that most hotels credit about one-third of the *en pension* charge to apartments and about two-thirds to food.

Where *bed and breakfast terms* are offered, either of the methods outlined above may be used.

Finally, it should be remembered that duplicate vouchers are not necessary in respect of meals included in *en pension* terms. Care must, however, be taken to ensure that a voucher is raised in respect of all other credit sales to *en pension* guests.

Functions

Most smaller hotels record functions sales in the visitors' ledger. The procedure is as follows:

(1) All particulars of functions sales are entered in a vertical column, headed 'functions', specially provided for that purpose. Thus, if a function were sold, consisting of 20 dinners at £1.00 and drinks to the value of £10.00, in the 'functions' column we would enter £20.00 against 'dinners' and £10.00 against 'liquors'.

(2) All such functions sales will be totalled in the daily summary column and included in the daily transfers to the monthly summary sheet.

Any amounts remaining unpaid by the organizers of such functions would have to be noted. Often a special 'functions diary' is kept and any unpaid accounts noted down in it. The treatment of functions in the visitors' ledger is illustrated in the specimen on p. 53.

Chance trade

Chance trade is a term applied to cash sales to non-residents. It follows, therefore, that the total of chance sales must be equal to the total of cash received. The treatment of chance trade is similar to that of functions, and may be described as follows:

(1) Particulars of all meals, etc., sold to chance customers are summarized, meal by meal, in what is known as the 'chance book'. This requires no special ruling and is kept for the sole purpose of summarizing all such sales prior to their entry in the visitors' ledger.

(2) The totals of chance luncheons, dinners, etc., from the chance book are then debited in the 'chance' column of the visitors' ledger.

(3) From the visitors' ledger the daily chance sales are transferred to the monthly summary sheet in the usual manner.

The 'chance' column should be balanced each day to ensure that the total of cash received and credited in the 'chance' column is equal to the sales debited therein. The treatment of chance sales is illustrated in the specimen given on p. 53.

Other forms of visitors' ledger

So far we have considered one type of visitors' ledger. Several different kinds of visitors' ledger are, however, used in practice. Yet, it is possible to distinguish two main types of visitors' ledger, and these are dealt with below:

Vertical visitors' ledger

This is the type already described and illustrated on p. 42. It is known as the vertical type because all charges to visitors are recorded vertically; also each visitor's account appears vertically—the upper portion being the debit and the lower portion the credit side of the visitor's account.

Horizontal visitors' ledger

In this type of ledger all charges to visitors are recorded horizontally and the names of guests are recorded vertically. It will be realized that there is, in fact, little difference between the vertical and the horizontal types of visitors' ledger. The difference is one of layout only. A specimen example is given in Figure 51, and students should compare this with the vertical visitors' ledger in Figure 41. In order to facilitate comparison, identical information was used to write up both ledgers.

Finally, there is a variant of the vertical type already described. The layout of this ledger is the same as that of the vertical type except that the daily sales are (a) accumulated monthly in the visitors' ledger, and (b) posted to appropriate ledger accounts at the end of each month.

It will be appreciated that, as a result, no monthly summary sheet is required with this type of visitors' ledger. A specimen is given overleaf. Two additional columns 'functions' and 'chance trade' are inserted to illustrate the treatment of these sales in the visitors' ledger.

Some basic considerations

A review of the various methods of accounting for sales outlined in this chapter suggests that in each hotel and catering establishment there are several ways in which it is possible to record sales. It will not be out of place, therefore, to conclude this chapter with a few basic considerations that influence the actual sales accounting records kept.

An important decision that must be made in each hotel is whether the hotel visitors' ledger should be used:

(i) to record all the sales of the hotel, or
(ii) to record sales to guests only.

Most smaller hotels use the visitors' ledger as a record of all the sales. Large hotels, on the other hand, tend to use it as a record of sales to guests only. Other sales (banqueting, bars, dinner parties, etc.) are then recorded in separate books of account.

Secondly, it is necessary to decide on the type of hotel visitors' ledger to be used, i.e. vertical or horizontal. It seems that the vertical type is the more popular. Further, the layout of the vertical visitors' ledger is such as to enable the individual guest's account to be more easily balanced than is the case with the horizontal type. Similarly, at the end of the day when both the visitors' ledger and the guests' bills are written up, a comparison of the two sets of balances and the location of errors seems to be easier with the vertical type of visitors' ledger.

HOTEL VISITORS'

Room No.	Name	Balances B/Fwd.	Apart-ments	Break-fasts	E.M. Teas	Luncheons	A/noon Teas	Dinners
1	Fenton	3 50	1 50	25	10		15	
2	Black	6 70	1 50	25		60		
3	James	7 60	2 50	50		1 55	30	
4	Stein	1 95	2 50	50	20	1 70		2
5	Dewey	2 30	1 50	25	10	75	15	
6	Saxton	8 90	2 50	50		1 80	30	2
7	Turner	9 80		50				
8	Weston	14 30		25				
9	Bentley		1 50			70	15	
		55 05	13 50	3 00	40	7 10	1 05	7

Figure 51 Hotel visitors' ledger (horizontal type)

Room No.	1	2	3	4	5	6
Name	Coles	Mills	Gordon	Bingley	Gallagher	French
Balances b/f.	10 40	4 50	16 70	2 75	9 70	11 90
Apartments		2 00		2 00	3 50	3 50
Breakfasts		50	25		25	50
E.M. Teas		30		30	15	
Luncheons	2 00		75		1 75	
Drink		85		2 10	30	1 75
A/Noon Teas			25		25	
Dinners				1 95		
Telephone		10			10	
Miscellaneous				50		
Paid Out			50			1 00
Total Debits	14 15	8 25	22 05	5 70	15 55	18 65
Cash	14 15					
Ledger			22 05			
Allowances					30	
Balances c/f		8 25		5 70	15 25	18 65
Total Credits	14 15	8 25	22 05	5 70	15 55	18 65

Figure 52 Hotel visitors' ledger (vertical type—alternative form)

LEDGER (horizontal type)

Liquors	Telephone	Paid Out	Miscel-laneous	Total Debits	Cash	Ledger	Allowance	Balance c/Fwd.	Total Credits
		05	40	6 80				6 80	6 80
60	15			10 75				10 75	10 75
		50		12 95				12 95	12 95
80	40			10 15				10 15	10 15
	05			5 60			50	5 10	5 60
1 20		1 80	50	19 25				19 25	19 25
				10 30		10 30			10 30
				14 55	14 55				14 55
20			1 25	4 65				4 65	4 65
2 80	60	2 35	2 15	95 00	14 55	10 30	50	69 65	95 00

7 Davison	8 Hagen	9 Brown	10 Beeson	Chance Trade	Functions	Daily Total	Brought Forward	Carried Forward
5 50	5 85					67 30	61 20	128 50
2 00	2 00	3 50	2 00			20 50	19 50	40 00
25	25					3 00	2 75	5 75
	15					90	1 05	1 95
	1 25			10 00	18 00	33 75	36 25	70 00
		1 00		4 00	7 00	17 00	15 75	32 75
25	25			5 00		6 00	4 50	10 50
95		3 50	1 20	16 00	25 00	48 60	41 45	90 05
			30			50	1 55	2 05
25		25				1 00	50	1 50
						1 50	2 50	4 00
9 20	9 75	8 25	3 50	35 00	50 00	200 05	187 00	387 05
				35 00	50 00	99 15	78 70	177 85
						22 05	40 00	62 05
						30	1 00	1 30
9 20	9 75	8 25	3 50			78 55	67 30	145 85
9 20	9 75	8 25	3 50	35 00	50 00	200 05	187 00	387 05

53

Finally, the degree of analysis of charges and the degree of detail necessary should be considered. Thus, where there are numerous minor selling departments it is necessary to decide whether the sales of each such department should be recorded separately, or whether some of them may be lumped together and, for accounting purposes, treated as 'sundry sales'. A similar problem arises in the treatment of functions. The treatment of functions, as described in this chapter, is rather simplified, and many hotels prefer to record these in greater detail. A common arrangement is not to have just one 'functions' column in the visitors' ledger but to make several columns available for this purpose. The sales in respect of each function would thus be recorded separately.

Problems

1 Describe the two main types of the visitors' ledger.

2 Explain how double entry is completed in respect of the following: (a) charges to visitors; (b) allowances; (c) cash received from visitors; and (d) visitors' disbursements.

3 Write short explanatory notes on the book-keeping treatment of: (a) *en pension* terms; (b) advance deposits.

4 Explain how the following charges to visitors originate and how they are debited in their accounts in the visitors' ledger: (a) apartments; (b) meals; (c) drinks; and (d) sundry sales.

5 Peter Fraine is a proprietor of a restaurant. The following balances appeared in his ledger on 1st January, 19...

	Dr. £	Cr. £
Capital		12 000
Cash at bank	2 000	
Premises	6 000	
Furniture	1 500	
Equipment	2 000	
Food stocks	500	
	£12 000	£12 000

Open the necessary accounts and enter the above balances.
Fraine's transactions in January were:

January	1	Food purchases—by cheque	£96
,,	2	Paid by cheque for advertising	50
,,	4	Cash sales—banked	87
,,	5	Credit sales: E.X. Dining Club	22
		Midland Cars Ltd	12
		City Banking Co.	26
,,	6	Paid wages by cheque	69
,,	9	Paid by cheque for new furniture	150
,,	10	Cash sales—banked	93
,,	13	Paid by cheque for fruit	10
,,	16	Credit sales: City Banking Co.	17
		E.X. Dining 'Club	12
		Midland Cars Ltd	39

				£
January,	19	Paid wages by cheque		72
,,	22	Paid by cheque for fish and poultry		19
,,	26	Cash sales—banked		100
,,	27	Credit sales: Midland Cars Ltd		16
			E.X. Dining Club	19
,,	29	Paid for travelling expenses by cheque		12
,,	31	Paid wages by cheque		66

Write up Fraine's books in respect of January and extract his trial balance as at 31st January, 19...

6 Before business is commenced in the Hyview Hotel on 4th May, 19.., the cash book balance is £7.90 and the following balances are brought forward on the visitors' ledger from previous day:

Room No.	1	2	3	4	5	Total
No. of visitors	one	one	two	two		six
Balance b/f	£2.50	£4.75	£3.95	£10.90		£22.10

During the day the business is as follows:

Breakfast: all residents
Lunch: all residents in rooms 2, 3, and 4
Sherry: room 1—17½p
Departure: room 2—account paid in cash
Dinner: room 1; 1 only in room 3; 1 only in room 4
Wine: one bottle @ £1.25 served in room 3
Apartments: charged to all residents

Hotel Tariff

Apartments — £1.50 per person per day
Breakfast — 20p
Lunch — 50p
Dinner — 60p

MONTHLY SUMMARY SHEET				MAY, 19..		
Date	Apartments	Breakfasts	Luncheons	Dinners	Miscellaneous	Total
May 1	4.50	0.80	1.70	2.10	0.90	10.00
,, 2	6.00	0.60	0.85	2.10	0.20	9.75
,, 3	6.00	1.00	0.85	1.05	1.35	10.25

You are required:
(a) to write up the visitors' ledger for 4th May, 19.., in conjunction with a simple cash book;
(b) to balance the visitors' ledger and the cash book;
(c) to enter the day's business in the monthly summary sheet;
(d) to construct a trial balance as on 4th May, 19...

7 The following exercise on the visitors' ledger extends over three days. The follow ing is the tariff of the hotel.

Bed and breakfast			Rooms	
Single	— A	£1.50	1 —	6
Single	— B	£1.25	7 —	12
Double	— A	£2.75	13 —	18
Double	— B	£2.25	19 —	24

Extra child's bed in the room and breakfast — 75p
Early morning tea — 5p
Luncheon — 40p
Afternoon tea — 20p
Dinner — 60p
Coffees — 10p
Note: Breakfast is charged for whether taken or not.

First day
Arrivals a.m.

	Room	1 —	Mr J. Derbyshire
	,,	2 —	Miss L. Smith
	,,	3 —	Miss R. Fletcher
	,,	7 —	Mr F. Betts
	,,	8 —	Mr S. Stanford
	,,	14 —	Capt. & Mrs J. Wright
	,,	16 —	Mr & Mrs K. Booth

Luncheons   All arrivals
Arrivals p.m.

	Room	4 —	Rev. J. Smart
	,,	10 —	Miss S. Lake
	,,	17 —	Mr & Mrs Spencer
	,,	21 —	Mr & Mrs. F. Donaldson
	,,	22 —	F/Lt & Mrs Phipps

Afternoon teas   Rooms 14, 16, 4, 10, 17, 21, 22
Dinner   ,,   2, 3, 7, 8, 16, 17, 21, 22
Coffees   ,,   14, 16, 4, 10
Telephones   ,,   2 (5p), 7 (10p), 21 (5p)
Chance dinners   12 @ 60p

Write up the visitors' ledger and the monthly summary sheet and carry balance forward to the second day.

Second day
Bring forward balances from previous day.
Early morning teas   Rooms 3, 7, 16, 21, 22
Newspapers   ,,   1 (10p), 7 (5p), 8 (5p), 16 (10p), 17 (5p), 21 (10p)
Breakfast   All visitors
Departures a.m.   Room 1 — Mr J. Derbyshire, account paid in cash and closed
                      ,, 14 — Capt. & Mrs J. Wright, account paid in cash and closed
Morning coffees   Rooms 2, 3, 7, 16, 17, 21, 22
Arrivals a.m.   Room 5 — Mr F. Sandringham
                      ,, 6 — Mr D. Chalk
                      ,, 13 — Mjr & Mrs K. Jones and son
11 a.m.   Taxi   Mrs Spencer — 40p

(continued)

Flowers	Room 7 — 75p
Luncheons	Rooms 2, 3, 7, 8, 16, 22
Chance luncheons	18 @ 40p
Arrivals p.m.	Room 9 — Miss Thompson
	,, 11 — Col. L. S. Ward
	,, 18 — Mr & Mrs L. Hopkins
3 p.m. Theatre tickets	Room 21 — 80p.
Afternoon teas	Rooms 8, 10, 4, 17, 18
Chance afternoon teas	12 @ 20p
Dinners	Rooms 2, 3, 7, 10, 17, 18, 21 (1 only)
Telegrams	,, 17 (35p), 21 (65p)
Cigarettes	,, 3 (20p), 16 (30p)
Coffees	,, 8, 16, 17

Write up visitors' ledger and the monthly summary sheet and carry the balances to the third day.

Third day

Bring forward balances from previous day.

Early morning teas	Rooms 3, 5, 7, 13 (2 only), 16, 21, 22
Newspapers	,, 4 (5p), 7 (5p), 8 (5p), 11 (10p), 21 (10p)
Morning coffees	,, 2, 3, 13, 17, 21, 22
Departures a.m.	— Miss L. Smith, account paid in cash and closed
	— Miss Thompson, account paid in cash and closed
	— Rev. J. Smart, account closed and balance transferred to ledger
	— Mr S. Stanford, account closed and balance transferred to ledger
Arrivals a.m.	Room 15 — Mr & Mrs Jennings
Luncheons	,, 15 (plus 75p wine), 3 (plus 30p sherry), 21 plus 85p cigars), 13 (2 only)
Chance luncheons	12 @ 40p, also wines £2.25, spirits £1.10, cigarettes £0.50
Afternoon teas	Rooms, 6, 17
Chance afternoon teas	18 @ 20p
Departures p.m.	Room vacated 3, account paid in cash
Telephones	Mr Jennings 5p, Col. S. Ward 25p
C.O.D. parcel	Mjr Jones 20p
Dinners	Rooms 5, 13, 18 (plus 60p wine)
Chance dinners	12 @ 60p, also spirits 70p
Private party	Mr Samuel Johnson:
	10 dinners @ 60p, liquors £8.75, cigarettes 90p, account transferred to ledger

Write up the visitors' ledger and the monthly summary sheet.

8 The Lowcliffe Hotel maintains personal accounts for certain non-residents frequenting its restaurant.

The following were the balances owing from non-residents on 1st January 19...

Col. S. Merrick	£10
V. S. May & Co.	22
E. M. Browne, Esq.	13
Essex Plastics Ltd	32
Winter Sports Ltd	15

The following transactions took place with the above customers during the month of January.

January	1	Credit sales: V. C. May & Co.	£3
		Essex Plastics Ltd	4
		Col. S. Merrick	8
		Winter Sports Ltd	13
,,	8	Credit sales: E. M. Browne, Esq.	4
		Winter Sports Ltd	9
		V. S. May & Co.	5
,,	13	Cheques received from Essex Plastics Ltd	32
		Col. S. Merrick	10
		E. M. Browne, Esq.	13
,,	19	Credit sales: V. S. May & Co.	14
		Col. S. Merrick	2
		Essex Plastics Ltd	10
,,	21	Cheque from E. M. Browne, Esq. returned by bank, marked R/D	
,,	32	Credit sales: V. S. May & Co.	4
		Col. S. Merrick	5
		Essex Plastics Ltd	6
,,	28	Received cheque from V. S. May & Co.	22
,,	31	E. M. Browne, Esq. paid cash	13
,,	31	Credit sales: Winter Sports Ltd	9
		Essex Plastics Ltd	11
		V. S. May & Co.	8

You are required to: (a) write up the restaurant sales book and the cash book of the hotel; (b) post to ledger; and (c) balance all customers' accounts as at 31st January, 19...

CHAPTER 5

Accounting for other matters

The journal An important rule of book-keeping is that all entries relating to transactions should be recorded in subsidiary books prior to being posted to the ledger. Thus purchase invoices are entered in the purchases day book and then posted to the ledger. Similarly, copies of restaurant bills signed by customers are entered in the restaurant sales book and then posted to the sales account and the accounts of the customers concerned.

There are, however, several classes of transaction which cannot be entered in any of the subsidiary books already dealt with; all such transactions are entered in what is variously described as the journal, the general journal or the journal proper.

Let us assume that a hotel buys kitchen equipment on credit for £1 000. This, not being intended for resale, does not constitute the hotel's 'purchases' and cannot, therefore, be entered in the hotel's purchases day book. Consequently, a journal entry must be made. This is shown in Figure 53.

													26
			J O U R N A L										
19.. May	1	Kitchen Equipment A/c		Dr.	L 94	1000	00						
		X.Y.Z. Co. Ltd.			L 23				1000	00			
		Being sundry items of equipment purchased per invoice K.5.6794											

Figure 53

Note: (1) The account to be debited is entered first. (2) Every entry in the journal is followed by a brief explanation of the transaction. This is known as the *narration* and usually starts with the word 'being'.

When the entry in the journal has been made, it is possible to post the transaction to the ledger. Following the example, double entry in the ledger would be completed as shown in Figure 54.

													94
			Kitchen Equipment A/c										
19.. May	1	X.Y.Z. Co.Ltd.	J 26	1000	00								
						X.Y.Z. Co. Ltd.							23
						19.. May	1	Kitchen Equip.	J 26	1000	00	

Figure 54

As already mentioned, the journal is used for several types of transaction. Let us, therefore, now examine the main uses of the journal.

Journal opening entries

When, for one reason or another, a new set of books is being opened, the opening balances are journalized prior to being posted to the ledger.

Naturally, the occasions when journal opening entries are required are very infrequent. They are *not* necessary at the beginning of each accounting period, because the balances from the previous period are brought down.

Sometimes a business is purchased as a 'going concern' when, at the commencement of the new business, there are already in existence numerous assets and liabilities. A journal opening entry is then useful in that it enables one to calculate the capital of the new business easily and accurately before any ledger entries are made.

Example

On 1st January, 19. ., V. Bright commenced in business as a guest house proprietor with the following assets and liabilities:

Freehold premises	£20 000
Furniture and equipment	4 000
China and cutlery	500
Food stocks	100
Cash at bank	600
Creditors: A.B.C. Ltd	100
D.E.F. Ltd	100

The necessary journal opening entries are made and Mr Bright's capital ascertained as follows (**Figure 55**).

19.. Jan.	1							
		Freehold Premises	Dr.	20 000	00			
		Furniture and Equipment	"	4000	00			
		China and Cutlery	"	500	00			
		Food Stocks	"	100	00			
		Cash at Bank	"	600	00			
		Creditors: A.B.C. Ltd				100	00	
		D.E.F. Ltd				100	00	
		Capital				25000	00	
				25 200	00	25 200	00	
		Being assets and liabilities as at this date						

Figure 55

Credit purchase/ sale of assets

The credit purchase of an asset has already been illustrated, and a further example need not, therefore, be given. Sometimes circumstances arise which necessitate the sale of an asset, e.g. when the asset is being replaced by a new one.

Example On 19th March, 19. ., a hotel's restaurant furniture, standing in the books at £500 is sold on credit to Popular Catering Ltd. The entry necessary in the journal is shown in Figure 56.

19. . Mar.	19	Popular Catering Ltd. Dr.		500	00		
		Restaurant Furniture				500	00
		Being sale of restaurant furniture per Agreement dated . . .					

Figure 56

Transfers between ledger accounts

During the course of an accounting period, and particularly at the end of it, various transfers become necessary between ledger accounts. The need for such transfers may arise for a variety of reasons, but all such transfers must be journalized before any entries are made in the ledger.

Thus, during the accounting period it may be decided to write off a debt owing from a customer to a bad debts account. At the end of the accounting period it is necessary to transfer purchases, sales, etc., to the trading account, and all expenses and gains to the profit and loss account. All such transfers (known as 'closing entries') should be journalized.

Example On the 30th June, 19. ., it is decided to write off the following debts due from customers:

N. O. Penny	£100
V. E. Lusiff	£50

The necessary journal entry is shown in Figure 57.

19. . June	30	Bad Debts. A/c Dr.		150	00		
		N. O. Penny				100	00
		V. E. Lusiff				50	00
		Being amounts written off.					

Figure 57

Rectification of errors   When errors have been made in the entering of accounts, it is wrong to correct the errors by crossing out the wrong entries and inserting new ones. The correct procedure is to insert new, additional entries offsetting and rectifying the wrong entries. Three examples are given below to make this clear.

Example 1   On 1st May, 19.., repairs to furniture of £50 were debited to furniture account.

This is obviously incorrect as the furniture account now shows a greater debit balance which would suggest that the business has more furniture. To correct this error it is necessary to credit the furniture account (thus restoring the previous balance) and debit the repairs to furniture account to show that an expense has been incurred by the business.

Example 2   On 2nd May, 19.., a cheque for £100, drawn in favour of and sent to W. A. Smith, was debited in error to W. Smith & Co. Ltd.

In order to correct this error it is necessary to debit the recipient of the cheque, W. A. Smith, and credit the account which was debited incorrectly, W. Smith & Co. Ltd.

Example 3   On 31st May, 19.., the monthly total of the purchases day book was posted to the purchases account as £1 050 instead of £1 500.

In this particular case only one entry is necessary to correct the error; £450 more must be debited in the purchases account.

The journal entries necessary to correct the above errors would appear as shown in Figure 58.

19..						
May	1	Repairs to Furniture A/c Dr.	50	00		
		Furniture A/c			50	00
		Being amount wrongly debited				
		to Furniture A/c				
..	2	W. A. Smith Dr	100	00		
		W. Smith & Co. Ltd.			100	00
		Being cheque wrongly debited				
		to W. Smith and Co. Ltd.				
..	31	Purchases A/c Dr.	450	00		
		. . . .			450	00
		Being total on page .... in				
		Purchases Day Book £1500				
		debited in Purchase A/c as £1050				

Figure 58

Other uses of the journal   In addition to the four main uses of the journal we have already described, there are several others. The journal is used in partnerships on occasions such as the admission of a new partner and on the dissolution of the partnership. In limited companies it is used in connection with the issue of shares and debentures. In all types of business unit, the journal is used as a subsidiary book for transactions which cannot be suitably entered in any other subsidiary book.

Suspense account   Sometimes the trial balance may indicate that there is an error in the books, but it may be difficult to locate it without detailed search which may take a long time. In order to be able to proceed with the work a suspense account may be opened and debited or credited with the amount necessary to balance the trial balance. This may be necessary at the end of an accounting period when it is desired to prepare the trading and profit and loss account and the balance sheet of the business.

When the mistake is discovered, an entry is made in the journal which, when posted to the suspense account and the other accounts concerned, eliminates the balance on the suspense account and corrects the errors made.

Example   On 31st January, 19. ., the trial balance of the City Hotel showed the credit side to be £80 greater than the debit. The 'difference' in the trial balance was transferred to a suspense account as shown in Figure 59.

Figure 59

On 17th February, 19. ., it is found that:

(a) the monthly total of the restaurant sales book was posted to the sales account as £2 840 instead of £2 460, and

(b) a cheque for £300 received from the '64 Dining Club was debited in the cash book but was not posted to the club's account.

In order to correct the above errors and to eliminate the balance of the suspense account, it is necessary:

(1) to debit the difference between £2 840 and £2 460 (i.e. £380) in the sales account and credit it in the suspense account; and

(2) to debit the amount received from the '64 Dining Club in the suspense account and credit it in the club's account.

The three ledger accounts concerned are shown in Figure 60 as they would appear after the rectification of the errors.

The relevant journal entries are shown in Figure 61.

Suspense A/c

19..						19..					
Jan	31	Difference in Bks	80	00		Feb.	17	Sales A/c	380	00
Feb	17	The '64 Dining Club	300	00						
			380	00					380	00

The '64 Dining Club

						19..					
						Feb.	17	Suspense A/c	300	00

Sales A/c

19..					
Feb	17	Suspense A/c	380	00

Figure 60

19..							
Jan.	31	Suspense A/c Dr.	80	00			
		....				80	00
		Being difference in books					
Feb.	17	Sales A/c Dr.	380	00			
		Suspense A/c				380	00
		Being correction of monthly credit sales – difference between £2840 and £2460					
"	17	Suspense A/c Dr.	300	00			
		The '64 Dining Club				300	00
		Being cheque received, not posted to customer's account					

Figure 61

The trial balance   The objects and methods of extracting a trial balance were explained briefly in Chapter 1. It will be convenient, at this stage, to refer to the trial balance again and consider it in more detail.

The trial balance may be defined as a list (or schedule) of balances, both debit and credit, extracted from ledger accounts including the cash book and the petty cash book.

When a system of double entry is used, the total of the debit entries must be equal to the total of the credit entries in the ledger. As a result, provided that double entry has been properly completed in respect of each transaction, the two sides of the trial balance must necessarily be equal.

It must be remembered, however, that the trial balance is proof only of the arithmetical accuracy of the ledger entries. There are certain types of error that a trial balance will not disclose.

Omission of entries   If both the debit and the credit entry of a transaction are omitted, the trial balance will not be affected and the failure to enter the transaction will not be revealed.

Compensating errors   These are two or more errors which cancel out. When one amount is, say, over-debited with £50 and another overcredited with the same amount, the agreement of the trial balance will not be affected though there are two errors in the books. In the illustration on the suspense account given above, if the cheque from the '64 Dining Club amounted to £380, the trial balance of the hotel at the end of January would have agreed and the existence of the two errors would not have been disclosed.

Misposting of accounts   This error occurs when one of the entries is posted on the right side of the ledger but in the wrong account, e.g. when a cheque is paid to W. M. Brown & Co. and is debited in error to the account of Wm. Brown & Co. Ltd.

Errors of principle   This error occurs when, though double entry is completed, the posting is not in accordance with some accounting principle, e.g. when china is purchased by a hotel and this is debited in the purchases account. China is not 'purchases' in a hotel since it is not purchased for resale to customers.

Problems   **1** Write short notes on the uses of the journal.

2 On 1st July, 19.., J. Jones started in business as a restaurateur. His assets and liabilities were:

Premises	£11 650
Kitchen plant	2 450
Restaurant furniture	1 230
Glass and china	320
Stock of provisions	110
Cash at bank	1 020
Cash in hand	20
Creditors	430

You are required to make the necessary journal opening entry and ascertain his capital.

3 The following balances were extracted from the books of a restaurant at 31st December, 19..:

Purchases	£3 955
Sales	11 054
Stock of provisions	405
Debtors	994
Rent and rates	600
Wages and salaries	2 615
Light and heat	305
Repairs and renewals	201
Furniture	1 200
Creditors	500
Kitchen equipment	600
Plate and china	483
Cash at bank	1 967
Cash in hand	229
Leasehold premises	8 000
Capital	..

You are required to:

(a) arrange the above balances in trial balance form;

(b) calculate the capital of the restaurant.

4 Before extracting his trial balance, the book-keeper made the following errors:

(a) Transferred monthly total of discounts received, £25, to the debit side of the discounts received account.

(b) Credited two credit notes amounting to £12 to suppliers' accounts.

(c) Debited the cost of repairs to furniture, £48, to the furniture account.

(d) Undercast the purchases day book by £100.

(e) Debited H. P. Smith Ltd with a payment of £36 made to H. Smith & Sons.

State by how much the trial balance was out of balance by reason of each error and calculate the total difference between the trial balance totals.

5 By means of journal entries show how you would deal with the following:

May 1st   Received letter from A. Supplier stating that he cannot allow the £7 cash discount you had deducted when paying his account.

May 2nd   Cash purchases, £24, debited in error to glass and china account.

May 31st   Monthly total of restaurant sales book overcast by £300.

6 When preparing a trial balance of a restaurant, it is found that the totals differ. On checking the books, the following errors are found:

(a) The restaurant sales book has been undercast by £200.

(b) Bank charges amounting to £15 have been entered in the cash book but not posted to the ledger.

(c) A cheque for £50 paid to H.C.I. Supplies Ltd has been posted to the account of H. & C. Supplies Co.

The difference in the trial balance drawn up previously had been placed in a suspense account. What was the balance in the suspense account?

7 George Bacon is in business as a restaurateur. On 1st January, 19.., he decided to put his books on a double entry basis. His position then was:

Leasehold premises	£3 250
Stock of provisions	120
Loan from A. Penny	1 000
China and cutlery	115
Restaurant furniture	415
Debtors: A. G. Jones	20
G. M. Browne	15
Creditors: A.B.C. Co. Ltd	30
Wholesalers Ltd	80
Cash at bank	680
Cash in hand	20

You are required to set out the journal entry required for the opening of the books.

8 Jack Parker is in business as a café proprietor. On 1st January, 19.., he decided to put his books on a double entry basis. His assets and liabilities then were:

Freehold premises	£8 940
Furniture	530
Kitchen equipment	810
Cutlery and utensils	190
Creditors: X.Y.Z. Co. Ltd	50
J. B. Brown & Co.	20
Cash at bank	430
Stock of provisions	90

Set out the journal entry required to open Parker's books; open the necessary accounts and enter balances.

His transactions in January were:

January	1	Purchased provisions, paid by cheque	£100
,,	5	Purchased additional kitchen equipment on credit from Equipment Suppliers Ltd	200
,,	9	Banked cash sales	140
,,	12	Paid wages by cheque	45
,,	16	Paid Equipment Suppliers Ltd by cheque	50
,,	18	Paid amount due to J. B. Brown & Co.	
,,	20	Purchased provisions on credit from:	
		X.Y.Z. Co. Ltd	30
		J. B. Brown & Co.	40
,,	22	Banked cash sales	150
,,	24	Sold old furniture worth £50 on credit to the New Catering Co.	
,,	24	Purchased new furniture on credit from Furniture Dealers Ltd	400
,,	27	Purchased provisions on credit from:	
		J. B. Brown & Co.	20
		X.Y.Z. Co. Ltd	50
,,	29	Paid wages by cheque	45
,,	31	Banked cash sales	160

You are required to write up Parker's books (including the appropriate subsidiary books) in respect of January and extract his trial balance as at the end of the month.

CHAPTER 6

Mechanized accounting

We have, so far, considered the basic book-keeping records—subsidiary books and the ledger—by reference to conventional, manual methods of book-keeping. In fact, more and more book-keeping and related work is being done mechanically and relatively less and less manually.

A large number of hotel and catering establishments have already introduced various 'mechanical aids' in their accounts, control, and reception offices. A text-book of book-keeping or accounting would, therefore, be incomplete without some reference to 'mechanized accounting'. The term mechanized accounting is used in this chapter in a wide sense and includes any machine that is used to prepare basic accounting records* such as day books, ledger accounts, statements, payroll, and similar records.

The volume and variety of adding, calculating, and accounting machines increase yearly, and it would be impossible to examine all the types of such equipment and their respective uses and advantages. Consequently, we shall be concerned with the four main types of equipment—adding machines, calculating machines, book-keeping machines, and billing machines—in common use in hotel and catering establishments.

Adding machines

There are numerous models of adding machines available, but they all tend to fall into several fairly distinct categories.

First, there are *electric* and *hand-operated* machines. The electric adding machines are more expensive than the hand-operated machines. Whilst the hand-operated machine is actuated by pulling a handle, the electric machine performs the necessary operation by the operator touching a motor bar. Obviously the latter is the quicker and more labour-saving of the two.

Secondly, there are *adding* machines and *add-listing* machines. An adding machine has a number of keys, which, when depressed, cause the machine to add. The result of the operation then appears in the window of the machine. A disadvantage of this type of adding machine is that it does not provide the operator with a written record of what amounts have been added or subtracted by him, only the final result is available.

Most adding machines are add-listing machines. An add-listing machine has, in addition to the adding/subtracting mechanism, a roll or sheet of paper attached to it. Each operation performed is printed on the roll of paper. At the end of each operation it is possible to tear off the appropriate section of the paper roll, which shows the amounts that the operator has 'put into' the machine as well as the result of the operation.

Thirdly, adding machines vary with regard to their keyboards. Some adding machines have *full keyboards*, others *simplified keyboards*. A full keyboard adding

---

*Note: Since 'mechanized accounting' is concerned with the keeping of basic accounting records, it may be claimed it would be more appropriate to speak of 'mechanized book-keeping'. For the purpose of the present chapter, however, it may be assumed that the terms 'mechanized accounting' and 'mechanized book-keeping' (and, therefore, 'accounting machine' and 'book-keeping machine') are interchangeable.

machine has number keys from 1 to 9 for units of pounds, tens of pounds, hundreds of pounds, etc., and all the necessary keys for pence. A simplified keyboard adding machine has only keys numbered 1 to 9 and is designed for touch operation.

Whilst little training is required before using adding machines, the full keyboard machine is easier to master in the initial period. On the other hand, the simplified keyboard machine can be operated by touch more speedily after a brief period of training. A hand-operated simplified keyboard add-listing machine is shown in Figure 62.

Figure 62 Add-listing, simplified keyboard machine—Summa Prima 20. (Courtesy: Olivetti Ltd)

The adding machine can be made much more versatile by the use of a movable carriage, which will take wide sheets rather than narrow rolls of paper. An example of this type of machine is the *shuttle carriage* adding machine. It usually has two registers (mechanical devices for adding and subtracting) and enables one to add simultaneously two separate columns of figures.

The adding machine is a useful aid to book-keeping. It would be impossible to list all the uses to which it may be put in hotels and catering establishments. For example, it is useful in checking invoices, credit notes, and suppliers' statements; the casting and balancing of day books and ledger accounts; and accounting records such as wages sheets or the visitors' ledger.

Similarly, it is invaluable in producing daily and weekly returns on various aspects of hotel and catering operations.

Calculating machines Whilst adding machines are capable of adding and subtracting, calculating machines perform all the four basic arithmetical functions: adding, subtracting, multiplying, and dividing. In the accounts office a calculating machine is principally used for the last two functions.

There are numerous types of calculating machines, both manual and electric. In hotel and catering establishments smaller, possibly hand-operated, calculators are useful and have a number of applications.

In general it may be said that a calculating machine is of value where there is much multiplying and dividing to be done. With this in mind, several distinct uses of calculating machines follow.

(1) In checking invoices—to ensure that the number of units is multiplied correctly by the price per unit.

(2) In the valuation of stocks—to multiply the number of units in stock by the cost per unit.

(3) In foreign exchange transactions—to convert one currency into another.

(4) In the preparation of payroll—when it is necessary to multiply the number of hours worked by the rate per hour.

(5) In cost and control calculations—e.g. to arrive at the food cost per portion or the average spending per meal.

(6) In menu pricing—to arrive at the selling prices to be charged to customers.

From the application of calculators listed above it will be realized that even a small, hand-operated calculator is an invaluable aid to book-keeping. A popular model of that type of calculator is shown in Figure 63.

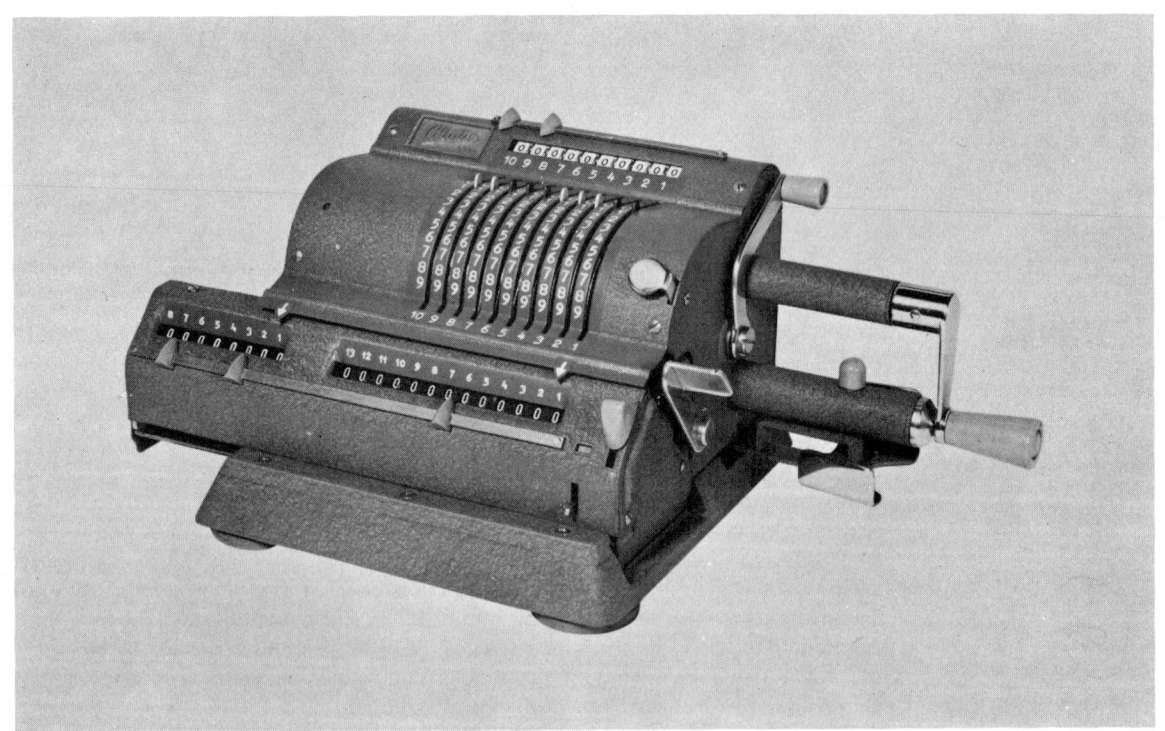

Figure 63 Hand-operated calculating machine—Multo Model 113. (Courtesy: Addo Ltd)

Accounting (book-keeping) machines

There are numerous types of accounting (book-keeping) machine. Some of these have developed from the adding machine; others have developed from the type-writer. Many are now a combination of the adding machine and the typewriter, as shown in Figure 64. Most accounting machines are very versatile and are capable of several different applications the most common of which are listed below.

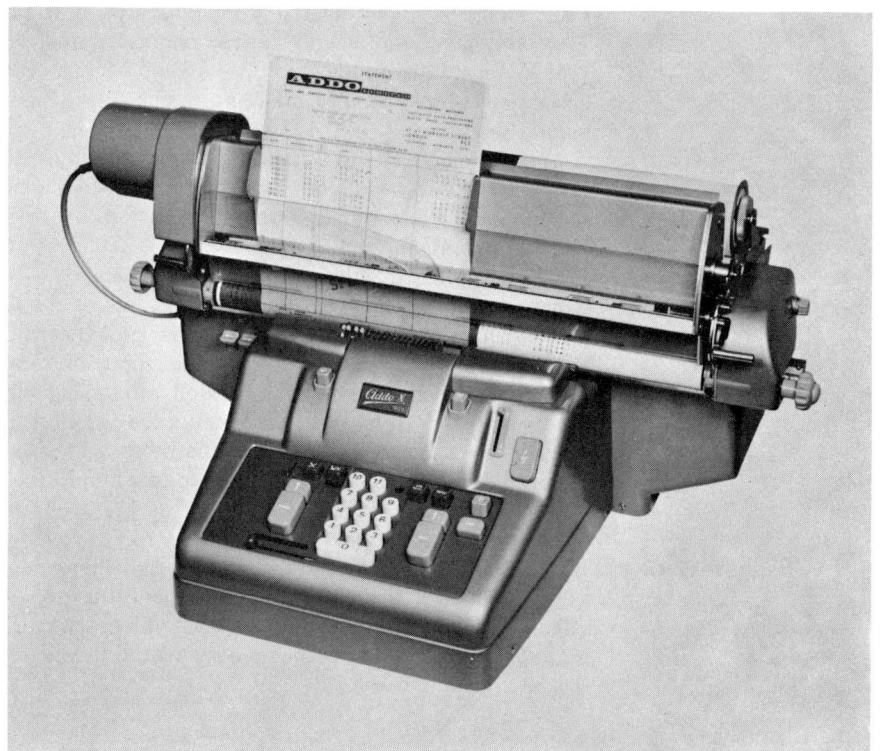

Figure 64 Electric, simplified keyboard book-keeping machine—Addo-X, Class 7000. (Courtesy: Addo Ltd)

Ledger posting

This is probably the most common application of accounting machines. Usually the accounts which are mechanized are the personal accounts, i.e. accounts of suppliers and customers. In order to be able to post ledger accounts by machine, loose-leaf accounts (rather than bound books) must be used. The usual procedure is:

(1) All posting media (suppliers' invoices, credit notes, copies of bills signed by non-residents, carbon copies of cheques) should be numbered consecutively and collected into suitable batches.

(2) Each batch of posting media is then 'prelisted', this is done by making a list of the media, usually by means of an adding machine. The strip of paper from the machine is known as a prelist.

(3) Next, it is necessary to withdraw from the tray (or cabinet) the loose-leaf cards of the particular accounts to which the posting media refer.

(4) Each posting medium is then entered in the appropriate account and the total of the entries made posted to the control account (see Chapter 7).

It should be pointed out that when the above procedure is followed no bound day books are kept. They are replaced by the prelist and/or proof sheets. A proof sheet is a large sheet which is fed into a book-keeping machine to provide a record of all entries made in the accounts concerned.

Payroll Most accounting machines are also capable of calculating the payroll of the business. This will normally take less than one day in each week; for the rest of the working week the machine will be used for other work.

When the payroll of a business is mechanized, the procedure is briefly as follows. A specially designed payroll sheet (wages sheet) is necessary. This will have the usual ruling but two copies (with a carbon paper in between) of it are necessary. The top copy of the payroll sheet is perforated and is subsequently torn into pay slips for insertion into the employees' wage packets. The carbon copy, which is not perforated, serves as an accounting record in the same way as the hand-written wages book.

The payroll sheet and a specially printed employee's deduction card are inserted into the machine and both are written up simultaneously. Thus, one operation results in three separate documents being prepared—the payroll sheet, the deduction card, and the pay slip.

An accounting machine with a full typewriter keyboard may also be used for writing cheques. Many businesses use sheets of cheque form, each perforated to give about half a dozen separate cheques. Underneath each sheet is a carbon paper and a second perforated sheet to secure a copy of each cheque written.

The sheet of cheque forms is inserted into the accounting machine and the date, the name of the payee, and the amount are typed in. Subsequently the individual cheques are separated and sent to the persons concerned for signing. The carbon copies of cheques are then available for posting to the appropriate accounts.

Receipt writing In hotel and catering establishments maintaining numerous ledger accounts for non-residents, an accounting machine can be used for writing receipts in respect of cheques received from such customers. The procedure is similar to that for cheque writing. The top copies of receipts are sent to the customers and the carbon copies used as posting media.

Stock records Accounting machines may also be used for stock records. When that is done, a separate loose-leaf stock card is opened for each item of stock. The posting media are suppliers' delivery notes and stores requisitions.

Few hotel and catering establishments have, so far, mechanized their stock records, but it is likely that this particular application of accounting machines will prove more popular in the future.

Other applications There are certain other applications of accounting machines, particularly those with a large number of registers. Many businesses use such accounting machines for sales analysis, cost analysis, and various statistical reports.

Hotel billing machines A hotel billing machine is an accounting machine used in the bill office of a hotel to prepare the accounts (and bills) of visitors. A billing machine, therefore, replaces the hand-written visitors' ledger. There are several types of billing machines used in this country; two popular models will be described here.

N.C.R. Class 5 hotel accounting machine This is a very popular machine and is now used in numerous hotels in this country. The machine is shown in Figure 65.

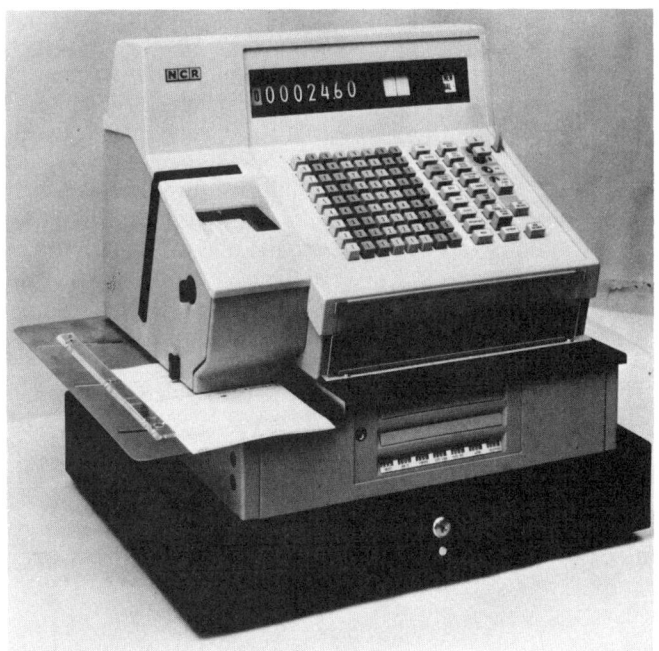

Figure 65 Hotel billing machine—N. C. R. Class 5 Hotel accounting machine. (Courtesy: National Cash Register Co. Ltd)

The posting media are the departmental vouchers, which must be issued by the various selling departments of the hotel every time a charge is incurred by a guest. A specimen departmental voucher is shown in Figure 66.

BAR CHARGE

NAME................... ROOM NUMBER 127

DATE... 15/2/71

DETAILS AMOUNT £ p.

DRINKS 40

SIGNATURE

Nº 773874

FORM No. 5/010B NCR 35957

Figure 66

During the course of the day the vouchers will be sent to the bill office. The bill office clerk will then take a given batch of vouchers, withdraw the relevant guests' loose-leaf accounts from the tray housing such accounts, and debit the charges to the accounts.

Each guest's account consists of two parts: the account itself and, attached in front of it, the guest's statement (bill). As the charges are posted, the two are written up simultaneously and no discrepancies between them are possible. After the posting of each charge the guest's account is balanced automatically. Thus, provided all the vouchers have been posted, each account is balanced and ready for presentation to the guest. When the account is paid by the guest, the amount paid is recorded by the machine and the top copy of the account (statement, bill) is given to the guest. The second copy is then filed. A specimen account is shown in Figure 67.

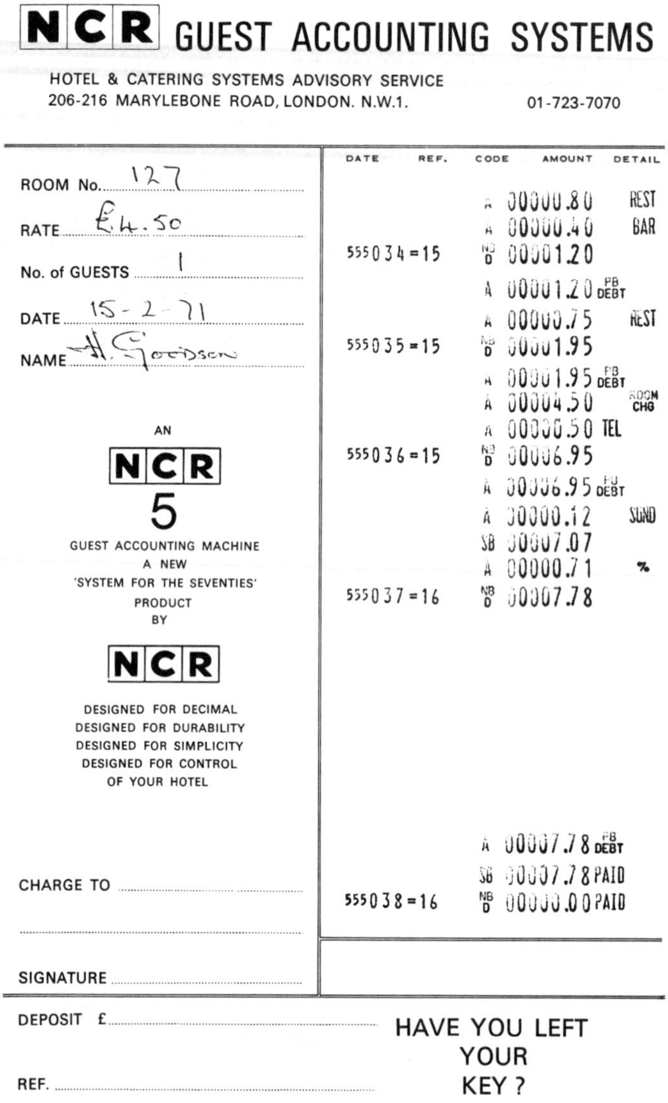

NCR GUEST ACCOUNTING SYSTEMS

HOTEL & CATERING SYSTEMS ADVISORY SERVICE
206-216 MARYLEBONE ROAD, LONDON. N.W.1. 01-723-7070

ROOM No. 127
RATE £4.50
No. of GUESTS 1
DATE 15-2-71
NAME H. Goodson

AN NCR 5 GUEST ACCOUNTING MACHINE A NEW 'SYSTEM FOR THE SEVENTIES' PRODUCT BY NCR

DESIGNED FOR DECIMAL
DESIGNED FOR DURABILITY
DESIGNED FOR SIMPLICITY
DESIGNED FOR CONTROL OF YOUR HOTEL

CHARGE TO

SIGNATURE

DATE	REF.	CODE	AMOUNT	DETAIL
		A	00000.80	REST
		A	00000.40	BAR
555034=15		NB D	00001.20	
		A	00001.20	PB DEBT
		A	00000.75	REST
555035=15		NB D	00001.95	
		A	00001.95	PB DEBT
		A	00004.50	ROOM CHG
		A	00000.50	TEL
555036=15		NB D	00006.95	
		A	00006.95	PB DEBT
		A	00000.12	SUND
		SB	00007.07	
		A	00000.71	%
555037=16		NB D	00007.78	
		A	00007.78	PB DEBT
		SB	00007.78	PAID
555038=16		NB D	00000.00	PAID

DEPOSIT £

REF.

HAVE YOU LEFT YOUR KEY ?

Figure 67

As the charges are debited to the guests' accounts, the billing machine accumulates separate totals of business done by each department of the hotel. The machine also accumulates totals of cash received from guests, allowances, transfers to ledger, and any adjustments. As a result, at the end of each day's business it is possible to prepare a daily trial balance, proving the accuracy of the day's postings. A specimen daily trial balance is shown in Figure 68.

DAILY TRIAL BALANCE

DATE...... 16 - 2 - 71 ....

	X 0024545 0	ROOM CHG
Department	X 00127.45	REST
Totals	X 00085.75	GRLL
	X 00076.42	BAR
	X 00027.25	ROOM SERV
	X 00015.50	GRCE
	X 00012.25	LDRY
	X 00008.55	SUND
	X 00028.50	TEL
	X 00011.75	PAID OUT
	X 00015.65	%
Sub-Balance	SB 0065457	
Less	X 00012.50	AD JUST
Less	X 00046.52	CITY LDGR
Less	X 00128.25	PAID
Sub-Balance	SB 0043730	
Add Brought Forward	A 0054552	PB DEBT
Balance	555054=16 B J0980.82	
Add		
Add		
Subtract		
Subtract		
Balance	055=16 B J0980.82	

		Transaction Counters
Summary Cards Up-dated	✓	
Audit Roll Removed & Re-connected	✓	I.
Audit Roll Locked	✓	2.
Date Changed	✓	3.
Zero Proof Printed	✓	4.
Register Locked	✓	5.
Detector Counter Reading	0101	6.
Signature		7.

NCR FORM No. S/001/A

Figure 68

The Sweda hotel accounting machine

Another popular billing machine (see Figure 69) is the Sweda Hotel Accounting Machine. This is similar in operation to other billing machines. The Sweda can be equipped with anything from twelve to twenty-seven analysis totals, depending on the requirements of the hotel concerned. All transactions with hotel guests are totalled and balanced daily on a machine-printed report. The Daily Report shows totals of cash received, an analysis of charges made to guests, commissions, discounts, ledger transfers, refunds and the outstanding debit and credit balances at the end of each day.

Figure 69 Hotel accounting machine—Sweda. (Courtesy: Sweda Ltd)

Restaurant billing machines

Most billing machines are used in hotels to maintain the accounts of visitors. A recent development, however, is the introduction of such machines in restaurants. The number of restaurants using such machines has increased considerably.

A restaurant billing machine is similar in construction and operation to a hotel billing machine. For instance, the National Cash Register Class 52 billing machine, shown in Figure 70, may be used either as a hotel or a restaurant billing machine.

Figure 70 Restaurant billing machine—N. C. R. Class 52. (Courtesy: National Cash Register Co Ltd)

RESTAURANT
BILLING AND CONTROL SYSTEMS

FOR
RESERVATIONS

206 MARYLEBONE ROAD
LONDON, N.W.I
01-723 7070

Table Number.........17..........   Covers......2...............

	--00.75 FD
	--00.50 FD
	--01.50 FD
EXPLANATION OF CODING :	--01.75 FD
	--02.60 DK
I. — FOOD.	--01.45 DK
	--00.30 SU
II. — WINES.	--08.85 SB
III. — BAR.	--00.80 %
IV. — CIGARS, ETC. 25 07	--09.65 TL
V. — SUNDRIES.	
TL — BILL TOTAL.	

25 08   --09.65 PD

NCR 32764   **TOTAL OF YOUR BILL SHOWN ABOVE**

SIGNATURE..

Figure 71

When it is used as a restaurant billing machine, the procedure is as follows.

The waiter, having taken the customer's order, prepares a food or a drink voucher in duplicate. He gives one copy of the voucher to the kitchen or dispense bar, and the second copy to the restaurant cashier. On receipt of her/his copy of the voucher the cashier files it according to table number. Thus each customer's vouchers are kept together.

When the customer requests his bill, a blank bill in duplicate is inserted in the restaurant billing machine and all vouchers entered on it. The bill is then totalled by the machine and is ready for presentation to the customer. A specimen bill is shown in Figure 71.

If the customer has an account with the restaurant and wishes the amount to be debited to him, he will sign the bill which will then be returned to the cashier.

The cashier inserts the bill in the billing machine and registers the amount of the bill as a credit sale. Subsequently, the top copy of the bill is passed to the accounts department for debiting to the customer's account. The second copy of the bill is retained by the cashier for filing purposes.

If the customer wishes to pay the bill, the waiter returns to the cashier with the bill and the appropriate amount of cash. The customer's bill is inserted in the billing machine and the amount recorded as a cash sale. The top copy of the bill is then returned to the customer and the second copy retained by the cashier for filing purposes.

Each amount entered on a customer's bill is analysed under appropriate headings by the billing machine. At the end of each day's business a complete analysis of all restaurant sales is thus available. The 'daily statement of business done' shown in Figure 72 gives particulars of all the sales of a restaurant as well as the division of the total as between cash sales and credit sales.

DAILY STATEMENT OF BUSINESS

DATE: 25/11/70

	NET TOTALS	CORRECTIONS	MACHINE TOTALS		
FOOD			25⅜ 34	−130.50	FD
WINES			25⅜ 35	−−95.75	DK
BAR			25⅜ 36	−−23.30	SU
CIGARS ETC.			25⅜ 37	−−24.95	%
SUNDRIES					
BUSINESS DONE			£174.50		
CASH RECEIVED			25⅜ 38	−154.50	PD
CREDIT BILLS			25⅜ 39	−120.00	CR

NCR 15926-R5005

Cashier...

Figure 72

Advantages of mechanized accounting

Mechanized accounting possesses several advantages. These vary somewhat from one type of accounting machine to another, and depend on the particular application of a given machine. Briefly, they are as follows.

Improved records

Accounting records prepared by machine are neater and more legible. There is, in consequence, less likelihood of figures being misread and so less likelihood of errors. This in turn helps in the balancing of accounts and in keeping them up to date.

The neatness of accounts presented to customers is extremely important. There is no doubt that machine-produced guest bills are neater and therefore more acceptable than hand-written bills.

Greater accuracy

Machine-produced accounting records are invariably more accurate than hand-written records. Often the records are designed so as to enable the machine to produce two or three records simultaneously (e.g. wages sheet, pay slip, and tax deduction card). As a result, transcription errors are eliminated. Further, the use of control accounts enables the operator to prove the accuracy of the postings more easily than would be the case with manual book-keeping.

Increased speed

Mechanized accounting also results in a saving of time. Most accounting machines have several time-saving devices such as automatic date printing, abbreviated description of items, etc., all of which save the operator's time.

Time is also saved by the simultaneous preparation of related records as well as by the elimination of transcription errors and quicker balancing.

Other advantages

In the majority of businesses mechanized accounting is cheaper than manual accounting. In a large business, employing several accounts clerks, the introduction of accounting machines may result in an immediate saving of labour costs. On the other hand, in smaller businesses no such saving of labour costs may be possible. Yet, even there, mechanized accounting may be justified because of the other advantages it has to offer.

Finally, mechanized accounting eliminates much of the tedious and repetitive book-keeping work such as casting, cross-casting, balancing, and checking. This enables the accounts clerks to spend more time on other, more interesting jobs.

Problems

1 Explain what you understand by adding machine; add-listing machine; and simplified keyboard adding machine.

2 List the main applications (actual or possible) of an add-listing machine in an establishment with which you are familiar.

3 Explain what is meant by a calculating machine. State briefly the uses to which it may be put in any one hotel or catering establishment.

4 It is proposed to mechanize the accounting, reception, and control departments of a large hotel. You are asked to suggest what equipment would be of value in

these departments, and state the main applications of each item of equipment. Make any assumptions you think necessary for the purpose of your answer.

5 Write short notes on the advantages of mechanized accounting.

6 Give a brief description of the operation and advantages of hotel and restaurant billing machines.

CHAPTER 7

Organization of accounts

Having considered all the basic accounting records—both hand-written and mechanized—it is now proposed to examine what may be described as the organization of accounts. The first considerations are the component parts of a full set of books, the relationships that exist between the component parts, and some related practical problems.

Divisions of the ledger

Though we often speak of *the* ledger, in practice this important book of account is divided into a number of separate sections. The most important object of division of the ledger into sections is to enable a number of clerks to work on the books simultaneously.

The precise division of the ledger is primarily a matter of convenience, and in practice the number of the divisions will vary from two (in smaller businesses) to possibly as many as ten, fifteen, or even more (in large businesses). Most medium-sized businesses tend to divide their ledgers into three sections, as shown in Figure 73.

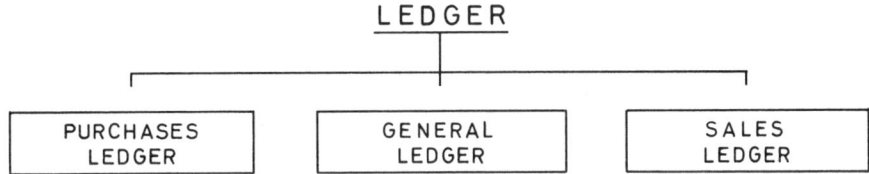

Figure 73

Purchases ledger

This ledger is also known as the bought ledger or the creditors' ledger, and contains the personal accounts of the suppliers (or creditors) of the business. It should be pointed out that the purchases account, though closely linked with this ledger, is kept in the general ledger dealt with below.

Whilst in the majority of hotel and catering establishments one purchases ledger is kept, there are some which divide it into several sub-sections. Thus a very large hotel could divide its purchases ledger into the following sub-sections: food, drink, tobaccos and sundries, and non-consumable supplies.

Each sub-section would then contain a distinct group of suppliers' accounts and might be in the charge of a separate clerk.

Sales ledger

This is also known as the sold ledger or the debtors' ledger and contains the personal accounts of the customers (or debtors) of the business. Again, it is pointed out that the sales account is not kept in this ledger but in the general ledger.

The meaning and nature of the 'sales ledger' must now be explained in relation to hotel and catering establishments. In such establishments the term sales ledger could be applied to two different sets of personal accounts.

It could be applied to the hotel visitors' ledger. This is strictly a sales ledger, in that it contains the personal accounts of the visitors. In practice, however, the visitors' ledger is not usually referred to as a sales ledger but as the visitors' ledger or the tabular ledger.

It could also be applied to the ledger containing the personal accounts of non-residents, any unpaid accounts transferred from the visitors' ledger and, possibly, advance deposits received from intending visitors. This ledger is usually referred to as the sales ledger, though there are many who describe it as the personal ledger. The latter is not an accurate description of this ledger, but is mentioned here in order to clarify the terminology in current use.

Most large hotels keep the two ledgers mentioned above. Some of the largest hotels might well sub-divide their sales ledger into two or three appropriate sections, such as non-residents, banqueting, transfers from H.V.L., etc., though it is not suggested that each such section would necessarily be looked after by a separate clerk.

Although many non-residential catering establishments maintain a sales ledger, it seems that the majority of them sell on a cash basis only and, in consequence, do not need personal accounts for their customers.

General ledger Whilst the purchases and sales ledgers contain personal accounts, the general ledger contains impersonal accounts, i.e. accounts other than those of suppliers and customers. Impersonal accounts are of two kinds:

(1) Nominal accounts—those recording gains and losses (or income and expenditure), e.g. wages account, rent account, purchases account, discount received account.
(2) Real accounts—those may also be described as property accounts, e.g. premises account, kitchen plant account, restaurant furniture account.

In many businesses the general ledger is sub-divided into two sections:

(1) Nominal ledger—this contains all the nominal accounts of the business.
(2) Private ledger—this contains all property (real) accounts as well as accounts of a confidential nature, such as capital account, proprietor's salary account, profit and loss account.

Subsidiary books In addition to the ledger or ledgers, a business will keep a number of subsidiary books. These are also described as day books, journals, books of prime entry, and books of original entry. The most important objects of subsidiary books are:

(1) To relieve the ledger of unnecessary detail. Thus, the periodical totals from the purchases day book are posted to the purchases account, which considerably reduces the number of entries in that account. Similarly, the periodical analysed totals from the petty cash book are posted to the respective accounts in the ledger, which, again, results in a considerable reduction of entries in the accounts concerned.
(2) To classify transactions and enable periodical totals to be posted to appropriate accounts in the ledger. To this end separate subsidiary books are kept for different kinds of transaction. There are the purchases day book for credit purchases and the purchases returns book for purchases returns. Also, there are analysis columns in the petty cash book for the different kinds of petty cash expenditure. As a result, it is possible to record different kinds of transactions in separate books. Once the subsidiary books have been written up, their totals (weekly, monthly) are available for posting to ledger accounts.

The most important subsidiary books in common use are listed below:

(1) Purchases day book	(5) Wages book
(2) Purchases returns book	(6) Journal
(3) Sales day book	(7) Cash book
(4) Sales returns book	(8) Petty cash book

Whilst the distinction between ledger accounts and subsidiary books is quite clear, there are several accounting records the nature of which needs a more detailed explanation.

The cash book, as indicated above, is a subsidiary book. Yet, at the same time, it is also a part of the ledger—though usually kept as a separate book. As a result, any transaction entered in the cash book (i.e. cash transaction) must not be entered in any other subsidiary book. Thus cash purchases are not entered in the purchases day book, nor is the purchase of assets for cash journalized. All entries made in the cash book count for double entry purposes.

The petty cash book is in the same category. It is both a subsidiary book and a ledger account.

The hotel visitors' ledger is, again, a ledger and a subsidiary book. It is a ledger because it contains the personal accounts of hotel visitors; it is a subsidiary book because it collects similar transactions (apartments, breakfasts, luncheons, dinners, telephone, and other charges) together and enables a daily total of each such group of transactions to be posted, *via* the monthly summary sheet, to the appropriate nominal accounts in the ledger. In the case of the vertical type of hotel visitors' ledger, the vertical columns are the ledger accounts whilst the horizontal columns are in the nature of subsidiary books.

Finally, the monthly summary sheet is another accounting record the nature of which is rather difficult to define. It is not a subsidiary book, in that it is not a record of individual transactions but one of daily totals, nor is it a set of ledger accounts. It is a statistical summary of sales, half-way between a subsidiary book and a ledger.

Subsidiary books and double entry

At this point, it is necessary to state briefly the following important book-keeping rule. *Every transaction must be entered in a subsidiary book before being posted to the ledger.*

The above rule will have already been observed from the illustrations given in the previous chapters. Thus purchase invoices are entered in a purchases day book before being posted to the purchases account and the accounts of suppliers in the bought ledger.

Hence the book-keeping process is a two-stage process: stage one is the entries in a subsidiary book, and stage two is the ledger postings. Double entry in respect of all transactions is completed in the ledger and no entries in subsidiary books count for double entry purposes. The student's attention is, however, drawn to the exceptional position of the cash book and the petty cash book as explained above.

Sources of entries

In practice it will be found that every entry made in the books of a business is supported by a document, e.g. an invoice, credit note, or petty cash voucher. All such documents are referred to as 'sources of entries' or 'documentary evidence', and are necessary for two reasons:

(1) To provide the book-keeper with detailed information regarding the transactions of the business. Clearly, in the absence of such information it would be extremely difficult for him to maintain the books.

(2) To provide the necessary evidence that the books constitute a true record of the transactions that have taken place. As a result, it is possible to support each entry in the books by some document and, in this way, prove that the books are a true expression of the transactions of the business.

It may so happen that no actual documentary evidence is available, in which case a substitute document must be provided. For instance, when a purchase invoice is mislaid and cannot be found, it is possible to ask the supplier concerned to issue a duplicate invoice. When an amount is paid out of petty cash and no voucher can practically be obtained for it (e.g. in respect of gratuities to delivery men, taxi fares, etc.) an internal petty cash voucher must be raised and signed by some responsible person.

The following is a list of the main sources of entries used for books of account:

Purchases day book:		suppliers' invoices.
Purchases returns book:		suppliers' credit notes.
Sales day book:		copies of bills signed by customers and copies of accounts sent to banqueting debtors.
Sales returns book:		copies of credit notes sent to customers; this book is not often used in hotel and catering establishments.
Wages book:		time sheets, clock cards, and similar records.
Journal:		various documents according to the nature of transaction, e.g. invoices in respect of assets purchased on credit.
Cash book:	Dr.	in respect of cheques received, copies of receipts issued to customers; in respect of cash sales, till rolls; in respect of all amounts banked, the paying-in book; also bank statement in respect of amounts credited by the bank.
	Cr.	cheque counterfoils or copies of cheques; suppliers' accounts and statements in respect of all payments made; also the bank statement in respect of amounts debited by the bank such as bank charges, bank interest.
Petty cash book:	Dr.	cheque counterfoils in respect of any floats received by petty cashier.
	Cr.	petty cash vouchers, external and internal.
Visitors' ledger:	Dr.	departmental vouchers (see Chapter 4) 'sources of charges'.
	Cr.	copies of receipts issued in respect of accounts settled; also monthly allowances sheet or allowances book in respect of allowances to guests.

It will be appreciated that, as there is some documentary evidence in respect of each entry in the books, it is possible to trace each transaction from the ledger posting to the original documentary evidence and *vice versa*. The following illustration shows the path of a transaction in respect of a credit purchase:

Order placed to supplier		**Order form**
Goods received by hotel		**Delivery note**
Charge made by supplier		**Invoice**
Purchase recorded by hotel	— stage I	**Purchases day book**
„ „ „ „	— stage II	Dr. purchases account
		Cr. supplier's account

Ledger folios

Reference has already been made to what are known as ledger folios. A folio is a page of a ledger or subsidiary book. Folio numbers are the page numbers of the ledger or subsidiary books.

In practical book-keeping, every time an entry is made a cross-reference is provided in the folio column to the corresponding entry in some other book. This method of cross-referencing has two advantages. In respect of each entry there is an immediate cross-reference to a corresponding entry in some other book, and the insertion of ledger folios provides a proof that double entry has been completed.

Two illustrations are now given to make the foregoing clear.

Example I, cash transactions

A cash transaction is entered on one side of the cash book and on the opposite side of a ledger account (Figure 74). The page number of the ledger account concerned is shown in the folio column of the cash book; the page number of the cash book is shown in the folio column of the ledger account.

		Cash Book									46
19.. Jan	1	Sales	GL 37	300	00	19.. Jan	2	Wages	GL 16	100	00
		Wages A/c									16
19.. Jan	2	Cash	CB 46	100	00						
		Sales A/c									37
						19.. Jan	1	Cash	CB 46	300	00

Figure 74

Example 2, credit transactions

Most credit transactions occur in respect of the purchases and sales of a business. As already explained, all such credit transactions are recorded in a subsidiary book prior to being posted to the ledger (Figures 75 and 76).

		Purchases Day Book			51
19.. Jan.	1	Supplier A	BL 24	200	00
"	8	" B	BL 16	100	00
"	23	" A	BL 24	50	00
"	29	" B	BL 16	150	00
"	31	Transferred to Purchases A/c	GL 61	500	00

Figure 75

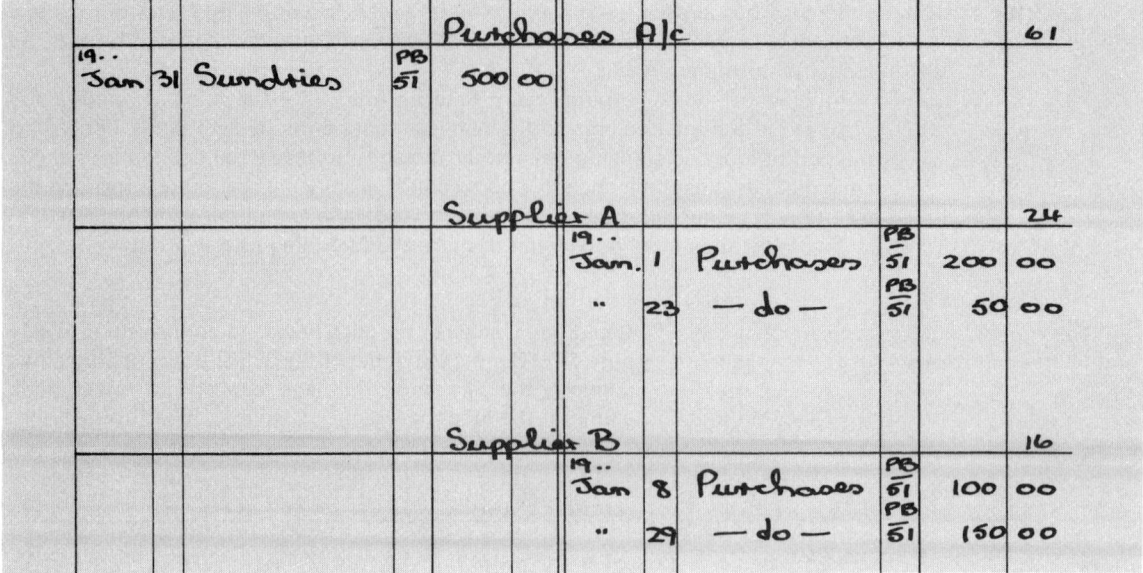

										61
				Purchases A/c						
19..										
Jan	31	Sundries	PB 51	500	00					

										24
				Supplier A						
				19..						
				Jan.	1	Purchases	PB 51	200	00	
				,,	23	— do —	PB 51	50	00	

										16
				Supplier B						
				19..						
				Jan	8	Purchases	PB 51	100	00	
				,,	29	— do —	PB 51	150	00	

Figure 76

The page number of the ledger accounts concerned is shown in the folio columns of the subsidiary books; the page number of the appropriate subsidiary book is shown in the ledger accounts.

The abbreviations G.L., B.L., C.B., and P.B. are in common use and refer to the general ledger, bought ledger, cash book and purchases day book respectively.

As explained in **Chapter 5**, there are certain transactions which are passed through the journal. All such transactions are folioed in the same manner as those shown in Example 2.

Control accounts

Another important feature of practical book-keeping is the maintenance of what are known as 'control accounts'. A control account is a device which makes a ledger 'self-balancing' by enabling a clerk to balance a section of the accounts (usually bought ledger or sales ledger) independently of the other sections.

In most businesses, including hotel and catering, it will be found that the largest group of accounts consists of personal accounts of suppliers and customers. It will be appreciated that, whilst the number of nominal and real accounts in a medium-sized business is not likely to exceed about fifty, the number of personal accounts may well run into hundreds.

When, at the end of an accounting period, a total trial balance is extracted and fails to balance, it is impossible in the absence of control accounts to determine immediately in which section of the ledger the errors have arisen. It is, therefore, often necessary to check all the accounts—real, nominal and personal: a process that may take several days.

A control account, by making a ledger self-balancing, enables the clerk concerned to determine at the end of each period whether or not his section of the ledger balances and, in this way, not only helps in the location of errors but reduces considerably the time spent by clerks on periodical checking of accounts and 'looking for errors'.

In order to understand the operation of control accounts, the following two points must be clearly appreciated.

(1) A control account is a *total account* and shows in summary form the detailed entries made in a particular ledger.

(2) A control account, though described as an account, is a *memorandum account*. Any entries made in a control account do not, therefore, count for double entry purposes. As a result, it does not really matter whether the entries are made in a control account on the same side as in the ledger controlled by it or whether such entries are reversed. In practice, when the control account is kept in the ledger concerned, the entries in the control account are usually reversed. This enables the clerk to extract what is known as a 'sectional trial balance'. When the control account is kept in another ledger (usually the general ledger), any entries made in it are usually kept on the same side as in the ledger concerned.

The following example illustrates the compilation of a control account by reference to the accounts of suppliers.

Example On 1st January, 19.., the following balances appeared in the bought ledger of a hotel:

Hotel Suppliers Ltd	£100.00
B. Brown & Sons	150.00
Holland Bacon Co.	50.00
	£300.00

If the hotel's bought ledger control account were kept in the bought ledger then, on the above date, it would appear as shown in Figure 77.

Figure 77

In January the hotel makes the following transactions with its suppliers:

Credit purchases:

January	2	Hotel Suppliers Ltd	£25.00
,,	4	Holland Bacon Co.	30.00
,,	7	B. Brown & Sons	40.00
,,	11	Holland Bacon Co.	10.00
,,	16	Hotel Suppliers Ltd	35.00
,,	22	B. Brown & Sons	55.00
,,	25	Hotel Suppliers Ltd	60.00
,,	31	Holland Bacon Co.	25.00
			Total £280.00

Purchases returns:

January	6	Hotel Suppliers Ltd	£5.00
„	18	B. Brown & Sons	10.00
„	30	Holland Bacon Co.	5.00
			Total £20.00

Payments to suppliers:

			Cheque	Discount	Total
January	20	Hotel Suppliers Ltd	£95.00	£5.00	£100.00
„	20	B. Brown & Sons	143.00	7.00	150.00
		Total	£238.00	£12.00	£250.00

The credit purchases and purchases returns are entered in the purchases day book and the purchases returns book and then posted to the ledger in the usual manner. In order to have the necessary information to compile the bought ledger control account, it is necessary to insert an additional bought ledger column in the cash book. Every time a payment to a supplier is made the total of cash and discount is entered in the bought ledger column. A specimen ruling of such a cash book is given in Figure 78.

Figure 78

Assuming that, by the end of January, all the transactions given above have been recorded in the books of the hotel, the personal accounts of the suppliers would appear as shown in Figure 79.

19..						19..						
			Hotel Suppliers Ltd.									
Jan	6	Returns		5	00	Jan	1	Balance	b/d	100	00
"	20	Cash		95	00	"	2	Purchases		25	00
"	20	Disc.		5	00	"	16	— do —		35	00
						"	25	— do —		60	00

19..						19..						
			B. Brown and Sons									
Jan	18	Returns		10	00	Jan	1	Balance	b/d	150	00
"	20	Cash	1	43	00	"	7	Purchases		40	00
"	20	Disc.		7	00	"	22	— do —		55	00

19..						19..						
			Holland Bacon Co.									
Jan	30	Returns		5	00	Jan	1	Balance	b/d	50	00
						"	4	Purchases		30	00
						"	11	— do —		10	00
						"	31	— do —		25	00

Figure 79

In order to prove the accuracy of the postings to the above personal accounts, the bought ledger clerk compiles the bought ledger control account, and takes out a sectional trial balance.

He compiles the bought ledger control account by taking the totals of transactions posted to the bought ledger from the relevant subsidiary books. Thus, by referring

19..						19..					
			Bought Ledger Control A/c								
Jan	1	Balances	b/d	300	00	Jan	31	Returns		20	00
"	31	Purchases		280	00	"	31	Cash + Disc.		250	00
						"	31	Balances	c/d	310	00
				580	00					580	00
Feb	1	Balances	b/d	310	00						

Figure 80

to the purchases day book, he sees that the total of invoices credited to suppliers in January was £280.00. The total of credit notes, cash paid, and discounts received is ascertained by reference to the purchases returns book and the cash book. The completed bought ledger control account is shown in Figure 80.

At this stage the clerk knows that, in the absence of any errors in the books, each and every entry in the personal accounts of suppliers is included in one of the totals he has entered in the control account. He, therefore, proceeds to extract a sectional trial balance, as shown below.

Sectional trial balance. Bought ledger—31st January, 19 . .

	Dr. £	Cr. £
Hotel Suppliers Ltd		115.00
B. Brown & Sons		85.00
Holland Bacon Co.		110.00
Bought ledger control account	310.00	
	£310.00	£310.00

As the accuracy of the postings has been proved, it is safe for the clerk to balance the accounts of suppliers and bring the balances down as at the end of the month.

Some further points The above procedure also applies to the personal accounts of the customers of a business, i.e. the sales ledger. In fact, many hotels and restaurants maintain sales ledger control accounts and prove the accuracy of the postings to such accounts before sending out monthly statements of account to the customers.

Control accounts may also be applied to accounts other than personal accounts, though in most hotel and catering establishments the scope for such applications is limited.

Finally, it is necessary to mention the treatment of certain non-routine transactions affecting control accounts, e.g. bad debts written off, legal expenses debited to customers, etc. It will be realized that any entries made in respect of such uncommon transactions will not be included in the totals of subsidiary books used to compile control accounts. It is important to ensure, therefore, that all such transactions are posted separately to the appropriate control account. The balance of the control account will not otherwise be equal to the sum total of the individual balances extracted from the ledger concerned.

Problems 1 Explain what is meant by general ledger, nominal ledger, private ledger, bought ledger, and sales ledger.

2 A large hotel keeps its ledger accounts in five separate ledgers: private, nominal, bought, sales, and visitors' ledger. You are required to indicate in which of the above ledgers you would expect to find each of the following accounts: freehold premises; rates; discount received; sales; M. W. Biscuits Ltd (supplier); Col. J. St John (customer, non-resident); repairs and renewals; capital; sales; W. R. Stillings (customer, resident); restaurant furniture; purchases returns; advertising; kitchen plant.

3 List the main subsidiary books. Enumerate their main objects. Explain the relationship between the subsidiary books and the ledger.

4 (a) What do you understand by the term 'sources of entries'?

(b) What are the sources of entries for the following:
> (i) petty cash book,
> (ii) purchases day book,
> (iii) cash book?

5 Explain the use of ledger folios in practical book-keeping.

6 Write short notes on the objects and advantages of control accounts.

7 On 1st June, 19.., the total amount owing to the suppliers of a hotel was £320. During that month the hotel bought further goods from its suppliers costing £350. Goods found damaged, £30, were returned to suppliers. Also, the hotel paid its suppliers £250 and received cash discounts amounting to £15. How much did the the hotel owe its suppliers on 30th June, 19..?

8 From the following information write up the sales ledger control account and the bought ledger control account of a restaurant. Assume that both accounts are kept in the general ledger.

December	1	Total bought ledger balances	£255
,,	1	Total sales ledger balances	514
,,	31	Credit purchases	316
,,	31	Credit sales	618
,,	31	Purchases returns	19
,,	31	Allowances to customers	10
,,	31	Cash paid to suppliers	201
,,	31	Discounts received	10
,,	31	Cash received from customers	414
,,	31	Bad debts written off	31

9 The Pronto Catering Co. maintains a sales ledger controlled by a control account kept in that ledger. From the information given below, you are required to write up the sales ledger control account for three months, balancing it at the end of each month.

	January	February	March
Opening sales ledger balances	£450		
Credit sales	520	545	575
Allowances to customers	10	15	20
Cash received from customers	430	480	520

10 From the following information you are required to:

(a) write up the purchases day book and the purchases returns book;

(b) show the necessary extracts from the cash book;

(c) post the transactions to the ledger accounts;

(d) compile a bought ledger control account;

(e) extract a sectional trial balance as at 31st January, 19..:

Bought ledger balances on 1st January, 19..:

Wm. Butcher & Sons		£40
N. O. Nicotine Ltd		30
Catering Supplies Ltd		60
B. N. May Ltd		70

Invoices received:

January	1	B. N. May Ltd	£30
,,	3	Catering Supplies Ltd	46
,,	6	Wm. Butcher & Sons	22
,,	9	N. O. Nicotine Ltd	16
,,	13	Catering Supplies Ltd	8
,,	15	Wm. Butcher & Sons	21
,,	18	B. N. May Ltd	19
,,	21	N. O. Nicotine Ltd	11
,,	24	Catering Supplies Ltd	23
,,	27	Wm. Butcher & Sons	32
,,	29	B. N. May Ltd	16
,,	31	Catering Supplies Ltd	27

Credit notes received:

January	3	Catering Supplies Ltd	2
,,	12	Wm. Butcher & Sons	4
,,	19	B. N. May Ltd	1
,,	27	N. O. Nicotine Ltd	3

Payments to suppliers:

January	24	Wm. Butcher & Sons	£40 less C.D. £1
,,	24	B. N. May Ltd	70 ,, ,, 2
,,	24	Catering Supplies Ltd	60 ,, ,, 3

Having agreed your sectional trial balance, balance all personal accounts and bring balances down as at the end of January.

Maintaining a full set of books

The purpose of the present chapter is two-fold: firstly to illustrate the operation of a full set of books; secondly to give the student adequate practice in keeping a reasonably realistic set of records.

Two suggestions are, therefore, made. First, the student is encouraged to study carefully the example given below; in particular he should study the 'explanatory notes' given in the example. Secondly, he is encouraged to tackle as many as possible of the problems following this chapter. These have been designed to give the student sufficient practice in book-keeping techniques and to equip him with ability to keep a fairly complex set of accounts.

Example On 30th November, 19.., after eleven months' trading, the following balances were extracted from the books of the Atlantic Restaurant:

	£	£
Capital		20 000.00
Furniture	1 900.00	
Rent and rates	1 180.00	
Postage and stationery	135.00	
Sales		25 960.00
Repairs and renewals	995.00	
Petty cash	15.00	
Kitchen equipment	1 950.00	
Collector of taxes		65.00
Purchases	12 985.00	
Gas and electricity	1 210.00	
Advertising	1 730.00	
Discounts received		295.00
Glass, cutlery and china	395.00	
Miscellaneous expenses	85.00	
Wages and salaries	5 890.00	
Stock of provisions, 1st January, 19..	505.00	
Creditors: A. M. Grocer & Sons		160.00
Wholesalers Ltd		50.00
Devon Produce Co.		200.00
Quick Foods Ltd		100.00
Debtors: The '65 Club	35.00	
Agrarian Society	60.00	
S. G. Curtis, Esq.	15.00	
Wm. Brown & Co. Ltd	25.00	
Purchases returns		80.00
Leasehold premises	15 000.00	
Cash at bank	2 800.00	
	£46 910.00	£46 910.00

Open the necessary accounts and enter the above balances. During December, the transactions of the restaurant were as follows:

			£
December	1	Withdrew from bank for petty cash	10.00
,,	1	Banked cash sales	265.00
,,	2	Received invoices from: Quick Foods Ltd	80.00
		Devon Produce Co.	39.00
		Wholesalers Ltd	122.00
,,	3	Paid out of petty cash: fruit	1.00
		duplicating paper	3.00
		floor polish	1.00
,,	4	Purchased provisions, paid by cheque	95.00
,,	5	Restaurant credit sales: Wm. Brown & Co. Ltd	10.00
		Agrarian Society	25.00
		The '65 Club	30.00
,,	6	Banked cash sales	205.00
,,	7	Paid wages and salaries	130.00
,,	7	Tax deducted and graduated contribution on above	12.00
,,	8	Paid for new china by cheque	65.00
,,	9	Received cheques from customers: The '65 Club	35.00
		Agrarian Society	60.00
		Wm. Brown & Co. Ltd	25.00
,,	10	Received invoices from: A. M. Grocer & Sons	75.00
		Devon Produce Co.	50.00
		Quick Foods Ltd	81.00
,,	11	Banked cash sales	215.00
,,	12	Received credit notes from: Devon Produce Co.	5.00
		Wholesalers Ltd	3.00
,,	12	Paid out of petty cash: postage stamps	3.00
		vegetables	2.00
		gratuities	1.00
,,	13	Purchased groceries, paid by cheque	44.00
,,	14	Restaurant credit sales: S. G. Curtis, Esq.	5.00
		Wm. Brown & Co. Ltd	3.00
		The '65 Club	14.00
,,	14	Paid wages and salaries	128.00
,,	14	Tax deducted and graduated contributions on above	11.00
,,	15	Received invoices from: Quick Foods Ltd	19.00
		Wholesalers Ltd	64.00
		A. M. Grocer & Sons	65.00
,,	16	Banked cash sales	231.00
,,	17	Paid collector of taxes in respect of tax and graduated contributions due	65.00
,,	18	Paid by cheque for stationery	37.00
,,	19	Received credit notes from: A. M. Grocer & Sons	2.00
		Devon Produce Co.	4.00
,,	20	Paid by cheque for repairs	83.00
,,	21	Restaurant credit sales: Agrarian Society	12.00
		The '65 Club	13.00
		Wm. Brown & Co. Ltd	34.00
,,	21	Paid wages and salaries	149.00
,,	21	Tax deducted and graduated contributions on above	13.00
,,	22	Banked cash sales	395.00
,,	22	Paid for gas by cheque	54.00

(continued)

				£
December	22	Paid out of petty cash: flowers		2.00
		restaurant bills		1.00
		fruit		3.00
,,	23	Paid the following suppliers' accounts as at 30.11.19..		
		A. M. Grocer & Sons—cash disc. £4.00		
		Wholesalers Ltd	4%	
		Devon Produce Co.	3%	
		Quick Foods Ltd	2%	
,,	24	Received credit notes from: Wholesalers Ltd		2.00
		Quick Foods Ltd		3.00
,,	25	Received cheque from S. G. Curtis, Esq.		15.00
,,	25	Banked cash sales		205.00
,,	26	Paid by cheque for advertising		30.00
,,	27	Restaurant credit sales: S. G. Curtis, Esq.		10.00
		Agrarian Society		15.00
,,	28	Paid wages and salaries		133.00
,,	28	Tax deducted and graduated contributions on above		11.00
,,	29	Received invoices from: Devon Produce Co.		39.00
		A. M. Grocer & Sons		43.00
,,	30	Bank cash sales		299.00
,,	31	Paid by cheque for kitchen equipment		200.00

It is necessary to:

(1) write up the books of the restaurant in respect of December, 19..;
(2) compile a bought ledger control account and a sales ledger control account;
(3) prove the accuracy of the personal accounts;
(4) extract a total trial balance as at 31st December, 19...

(1) Restaurant books

Figure 81

19.. Dec.		*Purchases Returns Book*			16
Dec.	12	Devon Produce Co.	BL/3	5	00
"	12	Wholesalers Ltd.	BL/2	3	00
"	19	A.M. Grocer & Sons	BL/1	2	00
"	19	Devon Produce Co.	BL/3	4	00
"	24	Wholesalers Ltd.	BL/2	2	00
"	24	Quick Foods Ltd.	BL/4	3	00
"	31	Trans. to Purchases Returns A/c	GL/17	19	00

Figure 82

Explanatory notes (Figures 81 and 82)

(1) The invoices and credit notes received from suppliers are entered in the subsidiary books in chronological order.

(2) In many establishments the invoices and credit notes would be numbered and after posting filed consecutively rather than alphabetically. The numbers are then shown in the subsidiary books.

(3) Against each invoice and credit note there is shown a folio of the bought ledger account to which the document has been posted.

(4) Finally, note that the totals from the subsidiary books are posted to the ledger as at the end of the period concerned.

19..		*Restaurant Sales Book*			25
Dec.	5	Wm. Brown & Co. Ltd.	SL/4	10	00
"	5	Agrarian Society	SL/2	25	00
"	5	The '65 Club	SL/1	30	00
"	14	S.G. Curtis, Esq.	SL/3	5	00
"	14	Wm. Brown & Co. Ltd.	SL/4	30	00
"	14	The '65 Club	SL/1	14	00
"	21	Agrarian Society	SL/2	12	00
"	21	The '65 Club	SL/1	13	00
"	21	Wm. Brown & Co. Ltd.	SL/4	34	00
"	27	S.G. Curtis, Esq.	SL/3	10	00
"	27	Agrarian Society	SL/2	15	00
"	31	Trans. to Sales A/c	GL/18	198	00

Figure 83

Explanatory notes (Figure 83)

(1) As already explained, only credit sales are entered in the restaurant sales book.

(2) The sources of entries are the copies of customers' bills.

Petty Cash Book.

£. p.	Date		F.	Total	Food Purchases	Postage Stationery	Misc Expenses
15.00	19..Nov. 30	Balance	b/d				
10.00	Dec. 1	Cash Received	CB 1				
	" 3	Fruit	1	1.00	1.00		
	" 3	Duplicating Paper	2	3.00		3.00	
	" 3	Floor Polish	3	1.00			1.00
	" 12	Postage Stamps	4	3.00		3.00	
	" 12	Vegetables	5	2.00	2.00		
	" 12	Gratuities	6	1.00			1.00
	" 22	Flowers	7	2.00			2.00
	" 22	Restaurant Bills	8	1.00		1.00	
	" 22	Fruit	9	3.00	3.00		
	" 30	Travelling Expenses	10	1.00			1.00
	" 30	Vegetables	11	2.00	2.00		
				20.00	8.00	7.00	5.00
	" 31	Balance	c/d	5.00	GL 16	GL 11	GL 15
25.00				25.00			
5.00	19..Jan. 1	Balance	b/d				

Figure 84

Explanatory notes (Figure 84)

(1) The choice of headings for the analysis columns is primarily dependent on what expenses are actually paid out of petty cash.

(2) It is usual to enter each item of petty cash expenditure separately.

(3) It is important to remember to post the analysed totals to the ledger every time the petty cash book is balanced; also to show the folios of the ledger accounts debited.

(4) As may be seen from the folio column, all petty cash vouchers are numbered consecutively for filing purposes.

Cash Book

Date		F	Sales Ledger	Bank	Date		F	Bought Ledger	Disc Rec'd	Bank
19..					19..					
Nov. 30	Balance	b/d		2800.00	Dec. 1	Petty Cash	PC 14			10.00
Dec. 1	Sales	GL 18		265.00	" 4	Purchases	GL 16			95.00
" 6	– do –	GL 18		205.00	" 7	Wages & Salaries	GL 9			130.00
" 10	The '65 Club	SL 1	35.00		" 8	China	GL 4			65.00
" 10	Agrarian Society	SL 2	60.00		" 13	Purchases	GL 16			44.00
" 10	William Brown & Co.	SL 4	25.00	120.00	" 14	Wages & Salaries	GL 9			128.00
" 11	Sales	GL 18		215.00	" 17	Collector of Taxes	GL 8			65.00
" 16	– do –	GL 18		231.00	" 18	Stationery	GL 11			37.00
" 22	– do –	GL 18		395.00	" 20	Repairs	GL 12			83.00
" 25	S.G. Curtis, Esq.	SL 3	15.00	15.00	" 21	Wages & Salaries	GL 9			149.00
" 25	Sales	GL 18		205.00	" 22	Gas	GL 13			54.00
" 30	– do –	GL 18		299.00	" 23	A.M. Grocer & Sons	BL 1	160.00	4.00	156.00
					" 23	Wholesalers Ltd	BL 2	50.00	2.00	48.00
					" 23	Devon Produce Co	BL 3	200.00	6.00	194.00
					" 23	Quick Foods Ltd	BL 4	100.00	2.00	98.00
					" 26	Advertising	GL 14			30.00
					" 28	Wages & Salaries	GL 9			133.00
					" 31	Kitchen Equip.	GL 3			200.00
					" 31	Balance	c/d			3031.00
			135.00	4750.00				510.00	14.00	4750.00
19..									GL 7	
Jan 1	Balance	b/d		3031.00						

Figure 85

Explanatory notes (Figure 85)

(1) The object of the sales ledger and bought ledger columns is to accumulate totals for control accounts. Thus, by reference to the bought ledger column, it may be seen that the total of cash and discounts debited in suppliers' accounts in December was £510.00.

(2) The discount received column is in the nature of a subsidiary book; any amount entered in it does not count for double entry purposes. Whenever the cash book is balanced, the total of discounts received should be posted to the credit of the discount received account.

GENERAL LEDGER

				Capital A/c							1
						19..					
						Nov. 30	By Balance	b/d	20000	00	
				Furniture A/c							2
19..											
Nov. 30	Balance	b/d	1900	00							
				Kitchen Equipment A/c							3
19..											
Nov. 30	Balance	b/d	1950	00							
Dec. 31	Cash	CB/1	200	00							
				Glass, Cutlery a China A/c							4
19..											
Nov. 30	Balance	b/d	395	00							
Dec. 8	Cash	CB/1	65	00							
				Leasehold Premises A/c							5
19..											
Nov. 30	Balance	b/d	15000	00							
				Stock A/c							6
19..											
Nov. 30	Balance		505	00							
				Discount Received A/c							7
						19..					
						Nov. 30	Balance	b/d	295	00	
						Dec. 31	Cash	CB/1	14	00	
				Collector of Taxes A/c							8
19..						19..0					
Dec. 17	Cash	CB/1	65	00		Nov. 30	Balance	b/d	65	00	
						Dec 7	Wages Salaries	GL/9	12	00	
						" 14	— do —	GL/9	11	00	
						" 21	— do —	GL/9	13	00	
						" 28	— do —	GL/9	11	00	

Figure 86 Ledger pages 1–8. See note on facing page

			Wages and Salaries A/c							9
19..										
Nov.	30	Balance	b/d	5890	00					
Dec.	7	Cash	CB/1	130	00					
"	7	Coll. of Taxes	GL/7	12	00					
"	14	Cash	CB/1	128	00					
"	14	Coll. of Taxes	GL/8	11	00					
"	21	Cash	CB/1	149	00					
"	21	Coll. of Taxes	GL/8	13	00					
"	28	Cash	CB/1	133	00					
"	28	Coll. of Taxes	GL/8	11	00					

			Rent and Rates A/c							10
19..										
Nov.	30	Balance	b/d	1180	00					

			Postage and Stationery A/c							11
19..										
Nov.	30	Balance	b/d	135	00					
Dec.	18	Cash	CB/1	37	00					
"	31	Petty Cash	PC/14	7	00					

			Repairs and Renewals A/c							12
19..										
Nov.	30	Balance	b/d	995	00					
Dec.	20	Cash	CB/1	83	00					

			Gas and Electricity A/c							13
19..										
Nov.	30	Balance	b/d	1210	00					
Dec.	22	Cash	CB/1	54	00					

Figure 86 Ledger pages 9–13

Explanatory notes (Figure 86)

(1) The pages of the ledger are numbered, and it will be seen that similar accounts are grouped together: accounts 2–6 are those for assets, accounts 9–15 are those for recording expenses, and accounts 16–18 record the buying and selling of goods. In practice, one, two, or more pages of the ledger would be allotted to each account.

(2) Note how certain accounts collect totals from various subsidiary books.

(3) The balance of the purchases returns account is usually transferred to the purchases account before the preparation of the trading account. *(Continued)*

		Advertising A/c									14.
19.. Nov. 30	Balance	b/d	1730	00							
Dec. 26	Cash	CB 1	30	00							
		Miscellaneous Expenses A/c									15
19.. Nov. 30	Balance	b/d	85	00							
Dec. 31	Petty Cash	Pc 14	5	00							
		Purchases A/c									16
19.. Nov. 30	Balance	b/d	12,985	00							
Dec. 4	Cash	CB 1	95	00							
" 13	— do —	CB 1	44	00							
" 31	Sundries	PB 10	677	00							
" 31	Petty Cash	PC 14	8	00							
		Purchases Returns A/c									17
					19.. Nov. 30	Balance	b/d	80	00		
					Dec. 31	Sundries	PR 16	19	00		
		Sales A/c									18
					19.. Nov. 30	Balance	b/d	25960	00		
					Dec 1	Cash	CB 1	265	00		
					" 6	— do —	CB 1	205	00		
					" 11	— do —	CB 1	215	00		
					" 16	— do —	CB 1	231	00		
					" 22	— do —	CB 1	395	00		
					" 25	— do —	CB 1	205	00		
					" 30	— do —	CB 1	299	00		
					" 31	Sundries	SB 25	198	00		

Figure 86 Ledger pages 14–18

(4) The accounts are not balanced, as some would be transferred to the trading and profit and loss accounts. Others would require certain adjustments.

A. M. Grocer & Sons A/c — 1

19..						19..					
Dec.	19	Returns	PR 16	2	00	Nov.	30	Balance	b/d	160	00
"	23	Cash	CB 1	156	00	Dec.	10	Purchases	PB 10	75	00
"	23	Discount	CB 1	4	00	"	15	— do —	PB 10	65	00
"	31	Balance	c/d	181	00	"	29	— do —	PB 10	43	00
				343	00					343	00
						19.. Jan	1	Balance	b/d	181	00

Wholesalers Ltd. A/c — 2

19..						19..					
Dec.	12	Returns	PR 16	3	00	Nov.	30	Balance	b/d	50	00
"	23	Cash	CB 1	48	00	Dec.	2	Purchases	PB 10	122	00
"	23	Discount	CB 1	2	00	"	15	— do —	PB 10	64	00
"	24	Returns	PR 16	2	00						
"	31	Balance	c/d	181	00						
				236	00					236	00
						19.. Jan	1	Balance	b/d	181	00

Devon Produce Co. A/c — 3

19..						19..					
Dec.	12	Returns	PR 16	5	00	Nov.	30	Balance	b/d	200	00
"	19	— do —	PR 16	4	00	Dec.	2	Purchases	PB 10	39	00
"	23	Cash	CB 1	194	00	"	10	— do —	PB 10	50	00
"	23	Discount	CB 1	6	00	"	29	— do —	PB 10	39	00
"	31	Balance	c/d	119	00						
				328	00					328	00
						19.. Jan	1	Balance	b/d	119	00

Quick Foods Ltd. A/c — 4

19..						19..					
Dec.	23	Cash	CB 1	98	00	Nov.	30	Balance	b/d	100	00
"	23	Discount	CB 1	2	00	Dec.	2	Purchases	PB 10	80	00
"	24	Returns	PR 16	3	00	"	10	— do —	PB 10	81	00
"	31	Balance	c/d	177	00	"	15	— do —	PB 10	19	00
				280	00					280	00
						19.. Jan	1	Balance	b/d	177	00

Figure 87 Bought ledger

Explanatory notes (Figure 87)
(1) Personal accounts are not balanced before being agreed with the bought ledger or sales ledger control account.
(2) In practice, one or more pages would be allotted to each personal account.

SALES LEDGER.   1

The '65 Club A/c

19..					19..					
Nov.	30	Balance	b/d	35 00	Dec.	10	Cash	CB/1	35	00
Dec.	5	Sales	SB/25	30 00	"	31	Balance	c/d	57	00
"	14	– do –	SB/25	14 00						
"	21	– do –	SB/25	13 00						
				92 00					92	00
19..										
Jan	1	Balance	b/d	57 00						

Agrarian Society A/c   2

19..					19..					
Nov.	30	Balance	b/d	60 00	Dec.	10	Cash	CB/1	60	00
Dec.	5	Sales	SB/25	25 00	"	31	Balance	c/d	52	00
"	21	– do –	SB/25	12 00						
"	27	– do –	SB/25	15 00						
				112 00					112	00
19..										
Jan	1	Balance	b/d	52 00						

S.G. Curtis Esq. A/c   3

19..					19..					
Nov.	30	Balance	b/d	15 00	Dec	25	Cash	CB/1	15	00
Dec	14	Sales	SB/25	5 00	"	31	Balance	c/d	15	00
"	27	– do –	SB/25	10 00						
				30 00					30	00
19..										
Jan	1	Balance	b/d	15 00						

Wm. Brown & Co. Ltd. A/c   4

19..					19..					
Nov.	30	Balance	b/d	25 00	Dec.	10	Cash	CB/1	25	00
Dec.	5	Sales	SB/25	10 00	"	31	Balance	c/d	74	00
"	14	– do –	SB/25	30 00						
"	21	– do –	SB/25	34 00						
				99 00					99	00
19..										
Jan.	1	Balance	b/d	74 00						

Figure 88 Sales Ledger

Explanatory notes (Figure 88)

(1) See notes following bought ledger accounts.

(2) It is important to ensure that no statements are sent to the customers before sales ledger accounts are proved. This is achieved by means of a sectional or total trial balance.

(2) Bought and sales ledger control accounts

Bought Ledger Control A/c

19..				19..				
Dec	31	Returns	19 00	Nov.	30	Balances	b/d	510 00
"	31	Cash + Disc	510 00	Dec	31	Purchases	PB 10	677 00
"	31	Balances	c/d 658 00					
			1187 00					1187 00
				19..				
				Jan	1	Balances	b/d	658 00

Sales Ledger Control A/c

19..				19..				
Nov.	30	Balances	b/d 135 00	Dec.	31	Cash	CB 1	135 00
Dec.	31	Sales	SB 25 198 00	"	31	Balances	c/d	198 00
			333 00					333 00
19..								
Jan.	1	Balances	b/d 198 00					

Figure 89

Explanatory notes (Figure 89)

(1) In this case the control accounts are kept in the general ledger and, as explained previously, show in summary form the detailed transactions posted to the bought ledger and the sales ledger. Thus, by reference to the bought ledger control account, the total amount owing to the suppliers of the restaurant is, at the end of December, £658.00.

(2) The control accounts are compiled at the end of each period (week, month, quarter) by extracting the necessary totals from the relevant subsidiary books.

(3) As the balance of a control account is equal to the sum total of the individual balances in the ledger it controls, when extracting a total trial balance it is not necessary to list the individual personal accounts. Instead, the balance of the control account may be shown in the total trial balance.

(3) Proving personal accounts
The method of extracting a sectional trial balance has already been explained. In this case the control accounts are kept in the general ledger and the extraction of a sectional trial balance is not, therefore, possible.

The accuracy of the personal accounts may still be proved by listing all the personal accounts and their balances and agreeing the total of such balances with the balance of the appropriate control account as at that date. This method of controlling personal accounts is illustrated below.

Bought ledger control as at 31st December, 19 . .

A. M. Grocer & Sons	£181.00
Wholesalers Ltd	181.00
Devon Produce Co.	119.00
Quick Foods Ltd	177.00
Control account balance	£658.00

Sales ledger control as at 31st December, 19 . .

The '65 Club	£57.00
Agrarian Society	52.00
S. G. Curtis, Esq.	15.00
Wm. Brown & Co. Ltd	74.00
Control account balance	£198.00

It will be realized that whether one extracts a sectional trial balance or proves the personal accounts as shown above does not really matter. In both cases one is, in fact, agreeing a number of individual balances with the balance of a control account, which does not form a part of the system of double entry.

(4) Trial balance
Trial balance as at 31st December, 19 . .

		£	£
Capital account	1		20 000.00
Furniture account	2	1 900.00	
Kitchen equipment account	3	2 150.00	
Glass, cutlery, and china account	4	460.00	
Leasehold premises account	5	15 000.00	
Stock account	6	505.00	
Discount received account	7		309.00
Collector of taxes account	8		47.00
Wages and salaries account	9	6 477.00	
Rent and rates account	10	1 180.00	
Postage and stationery account	11	179.00	
Repairs and renewals account	12	1 078.00	
	c/fwd	28 929.00	20 356.00

		b/fwd	28 929.00	20 356.00
Gas and electricity account	13		1 264.00	
Advertising account	14		1 760.00	
Miscellaneous expenses account	15		90.00	
Purchases account	16		13 809.00	
Purchases returns account	17			99.00
Sales account	18			27 973.00
Cash book	1		3 031.00	
Petty cash book	14		5.00	
Bought ledger control account				658.00
Sales ledger control account			198.00	
			£49 086.00	£49 086.00

Explanatory notes

(1) It is useful to show the folios of the accounts listed in the trial balance in case any of them have to be referred to or checked.

(2) Should the trial balance fail to balance, only the general ledger accounts (including the cash book and the petty cash book) would have to be checked as the accuracy of the personal accounts has already been proved by means of the control accounts.

Problems   1 The following trial balance was extracted from the books of a restaurant as at 1st January, 19 . . .

	£	£
Capital		10 000
Premises	7 450	
China and cutlery	435	
Stock	215	
Rent and rates		25
Cash at bank	1 915	
Petty cash	10	
Gas and electricity		35
Creditors: A. Allen		50
B. Bailey		15
C. Cooper		45
Debtors: M. Maynard	35	
B.I.C. Ltd	60	
Midland Motors Ltd	50	
	£10 170	£10 170

The following were the transactions of the restaurant in January.

January	1	Paid gas by cheque	£125
,,	1	Cash sales	65
,,	2	Petty cash payments: fruit	2
		manager's fares	1

(Continued)

January	2	Cash sales	£55
,,	2	Credit sales: B.I.C. Ltd	5
		M. Maynard	3
,,	5	Paid A. Allen's account less 4% cash discount	
,,	5	Credit purchases: A. Allen	75
		C. Cooper	121
		D. Dawson	18
,,	5	Cash sales	81
,,	6	Purchased new china, paid by cheque	20
,,	6	Petty cash payments: stationery	1
		postage stamps	2
,,	7	Midland Motors Ltd paid their account as at 1.1.19. .	
,,	7	Cash sales	87
,,	7	Credit sales: B.I.C. Ltd	8
		M. Maynard	2
		B.S.A. Society	11
,,	8	Cash sales	53
,,	8	Paid wages and salaries by cheque	166
,,	11	Purchased stationery, paid by cheque	14
,,	11	Cash sales	65
,,	11	Credit sales: B.S.A. Society	9
		B.I.C. Ltd	3
,,	12	Credit purchases: A. Allen	37
		B. Bailey	83
,,	12	Cash sales	55
,,	13	Purchased provisions, paid by cheque	91
,,	13	Cash sales	88
,,	14	Paid C. Cooper's account as at 1st January, less £2 cash discount	
,,	14	Cash sales	62
,,	16	Credit purchases: D. Dawson	41
		C. Cooper	19
		B. Bailey	119
,,	18	Cash sales	71
,,	19	Credit sales: Midland Motors Ltd	8
		B.S.A. Society	7
,,	19	Cash sales	81
,,	20	Paid B. Bailey's account as at 1st January	
,,	20	Cash sales	49
,,	21	Balanced petty cash—drew cheque to make up imprest to £20	
,,	21	Cash sales	101
,,	22	Credit purchases: D. Dawson	55
		A. Allen	47
,,	22	Cash sales	76
,,	25	Paid wages and salaries by cheque	149
,,	26	Credit sales: B.S.A. Society	8
,,	26	Cash sales	81
,,	27	Petty cash payments: gratuities	1
		vegetables	2
		flowers	1
,,	27	Cash sales	64
,,	28	B.I.C. Ltd paid their account as at 1st January	
,,	28	Cash sales	74
,,	29	Credit purchase: B. Bailey	23
,,	29	Cash sales	69
,,	30	Paid out of petty cash: manager's fares	1

(Continued)

January	30	Cash sales	£ 88
	30	Purchased provisions from D. Dawson, paid by cheque	17
,,	31	Credit sales: Midland Motors Ltd	4
		B.S.A. Society	1
,,	31	Cash sales	88

You are required to pass the above transactions through the books of the business, extract a trial balance as at 31st January, 19.., close the cash book and the petty cash book and all personal accounts. Use separate sheets of paper for the main divisions of the ledger.

2 The following were the balances in the book of a restaurant after eleven months' trading at 30th November, 19...

Trial balance

	£	£
Capital		10 000
Stock of provisions, 1st January, 19..	310	
Sales		13 020
Purchases	6 530	
Wages and salaries	2 945	
Collector of taxes		35
Advertising	855	
Fuel and light	740	
Cash at bank	1 390	
Petty cash	10	
Repairs and replacements	485	
Restaurant furniture	900	
China, glass, and cutlery	215	
Miscellaneous expenses	75	
Rates	630	
Discounts received		145
Leasehold premises	7 400	
Kitchen plant	950	
Purchases returns		50
Creditors: Food Sellers Ltd		25
Dutch Dairy Co.		100
Catering Supplies Ltd		50
Oriental Foods Ltd		80
Postage and stationery	70	
	£23 505	£23 505

Open the necessary accounts and enter the above balances.

During December the transactions of the restaurant were as shown below:

December	1	Withdrew from bank for petty cash	£15
,,	2	Banked cash sales	35
,,	2	Received invoices from: Oriental Foods Ltd	15
		Catering Supplies Ltd	25
		Dutch Dairy Co.	20
		Food Sellers Ltd	18

(Continued)

December	3	Petty cash payments: provisions	£2
		stationery	3
		cleaning materials	1
,,	4	Banked cash sales	115
,,	5	Purchased cutlery on credit from Sheffield Cutlery Co.	175
,,	6	Banked cash sales	85
,,	6	Paid wages and salaries	76
,,	6	Tax deducted and graduated contributions on above	8
,,	7	Received invoices from: Dutch Dairy Co.	35
		Food Sellers Ltd	30
		Catering Supplies Ltd	25
,,	8	Banked cash sales	80
,,	8	Paid by cheque for provisions	72
,,	8	Petty cash payments: postage	4
		provisions	3
		cleaning materials	2
,,	9	Paid for electricity by cheque	90
,,	9	Received credit notes from: Food Sellers Ltd	5
		Dutch Dairy Co.	6
		Oriental Foods Ltd	4
,,	10	Banked cash sales	85
,,	10	Paid by cheque for stationery	37
,,	11	Purchased groceries, paid by cheque	74
,,	11	Received credit note from Dutch Dairy Co.	2
,,	12	Banked cash sales	83
,,	12	Paid wages and salaries by cheque	69
,,	12	Tax deducted and graduated contributions on above	7
,,	13	Received invoices from: Dutch Dairy Co.	20
		Catering Supplies Ltd	30
		Oriental Foods Ltd	40
		Food Sellers Ltd	10
,,	13	Paid by cheque for repairs	43
,,	14	Banked cash sales	79
,,	14	Paid the following suppliers' accounts as at the end of the previous month, and deducted discounts as indicated:	
		Food Sellers Ltd C.D. 4%	
		Dutch Dairy Co. ,, 3%	
		Catering Supplies Ltd ,, 4%	
		Oriental Foods Ltd ,, 5%	
,,	15	Petty cash payments: stationery	1
		provisions	4
,,	16	Banked cash sales	83
,,	16	Drew cheque for tax deducted and graduated contributions in respect of previous month	35
,,	17	Received invoices from: Food Sellers Ltd	23
		Oriental Food Ltd	13
		Dutch Dairy Co.	15
,,	18	Banked cash sales	88
,,	19	Paid for advertising by cheque	37
,,	20	Banked cash sales	61
,,	20	Paid wages and salaries by cheque	80
,,	20	Tax deducted and graduated contributions on above	8
,,	21	Received credit note from Catering Supplies Ltd	3
,,	22	Banked cash sales	83
,,	23	Paid out of petty cash for stationery	1
,,	24	Banked cash sales	89
,,	24	Received invoices from: Dutch Dairy Co.	47
		Oriental Foods Ltd	41

(Continued)

December	25	Purchased provisions, paid by cheque	£16
,,	26	Received credit note from Dutch Dairy Co.	2
,,	26	Banked cash sales	39
,,	27	Paid by cheque for kitchen plant	75
,,	28	Banked cash sales	37
,,	28	Paid wages and salaries by cheque	76
,,	28	Tax deducted and graduated contributions on above	6
,,	29	Invoices received from: Catering Supplies Ltd	16
		Food Sellers Ltd	39
,,	30	Banked cash sales	83
,,	30	Paid by cheque for kitchen fuel	45
,,	30	Sold for cash old cutlery	5
,,	31	Banked cash sales	82
,,	31	Paid by cheque for stationery	11

You are required to write up the books of the restaurant in respect of December, 19.., extract a trial balance and balance all personal accounts, the cash book and the petty cash book.

3 J. Robinson started in business on 1st January, 19.., with a capital in cash of £1 000, which he paid into his business bank account.

His transactions in January were:

January	1	Paid three months' rent by cheque	£155
,,	2	Purchased kitchen equipment by cheque	255
,,	3	Paid by cheque for cutlery and utensils	53
,,	4	Bought provisions by cheque	83
,,	9	Paid wages by cheque	31
,,	13	Banked sales	77
,,	16	Bought provisions on credit from X.Y.Z. Supplies Ltd	74
,,	19	Bought provisions on credit from A. K. Jones & Co.	46
,,	22	Banked sales	69
,,	25	Paid wages by cheque	37
,,	27	Bought provisions on credit from X.Y.Z. Supplies Ltd	38
,,	28	Withdrew from bank for private use	30
,,	29	Banked sales	107
,,	31	Bought provisions on credit from A. K. Jones & Co.	33
,,	31	Bought cutlery on credit from Catering Supplies Ltd	60

You are required to enter the above transactions in appropriate subsidiary books, post to ledger and extract Robinson's trial balance as at 31st January, 19...

(H.C.I. Inter. Modified)

CHAPTER 9

Simple final accounts

The most important purpose of any business is to earn a profit. It is, therefore, necessary from time to time—at least once a year—to prepare an account showing how much profit has in fact been made.

Similarly, it is essential from time to time to review the financial position of the business in order to see what assets or property it owns and what debts it owes to outsiders.

In order to ascertain how much profit (or loss) has been made and to show the financial position of a business, it is necessary to prepare what are known as the final accounts of a business. These are:

(a) The trading, profit and loss account which shows the income and expenditure in respect of a particular accounting period and the resulting gross profit (or gross loss) and net profit (or net loss).

(b) The balance sheet which, strictly speaking, is not an account but a financial statement showing the assets and liabilities of a business.

It is usual to prepare the final accounts from a trial balance, extracted from the ledger at a particular date.

It will be recalled that a debit balance may be one of two things: an asset or an expense. A credit balance, on the other hand, represents either a liability or a gain. Balances which represent gains and expenses are used in the construction of the trading, profit and loss account; those which represent assets and liabilities are used to construct the balance sheet. Students will find it useful to remember, therefore, that the balances from the trial balance are, so to speak, channelled in two directions: some to the trading, profit and loss account, others to the balance sheet.

Example   The following trial balance was extracted from the books of A. Caterer at 31st December, 19.., after a year's trading.

Trial balance as at 31st December, 19..

	£	£
Capital		15 000
Wages and salaries	5 500	
Rent and rates	1 700	
Repairs	800	
Drawings	500	
Creditors		600
Kitchen plant	4 000	
China and cutlery	500	
Debtors	300	
Stock, 1st January, 19..	400	
Sales		20 000
Restaurant furniture	2 000	
Freehold premises	10 000	
Light and heat	900	
Purchases	8 000	
Cash at bank	1 000	
	£35 600	£35 600

A. Caterer's trading, profit and loss account for the year ended 31st December, 19.., and his balance sheet as at that date are to be prepared. The following notes should be taken into account:

(a) At 31st December, 19.., the stock was valued at £300.

(b) The following assets must be depreciated:
    (i) Kitchen plant by 10 per cent;
    (ii) Restaurant furniture by 10 per cent;
    (iii) China and cutlery—this was revalued at £400.

(c) Of the £1 700 paid for rent and rates, £100 applies to the period following 31st December, 19...

(d) Light and heat due at 31st December, 19.., but not paid, amounted to £50.

Trading, Profit and Loss A/c for year ended 31st Dec., 19..				
Opening Stock	400	Sales		20 000
Purchases	8 000			
	8 400			
Less Closing Stock	300			
Cost of Sales	8100			
Gross Profit c/d	11900			
	20 000			20 000
Wages and Salaries	5500	Gross Profit b/d		11900
Rent and Rates	1600			
Repairs	800			
Light and Heat	950			
Depreciation :				
Kitchen Plant 400				
Restaurant Furniture 200				
China and Cutlery 100	700			
Net Profit	2350			
	11900			11900

Figure 90

Notes on trading, profit and loss account

As may be seen from Figure 90, the trading, profit and loss account consists of two sections. The upper section, which is the trading account, shows the gross profit; the lower section, which is the profit and loss account, shows the net profit earned by the business.

Gross profit is the difference between net sales (i.e. sales less allowances, if any) and the cost of sales. The cost of sales is arrived at by adding to opening stock the purchases for the year and deducting the closing stock in existence at the end of the year.

Net profit is the profit remaining after deducting the expenses of running a business from the gross profit. Hence, all expenses such as rent, rates, wages and salaries, depreciation, etc., must be deducted from the gross profit to arrive at the net profit.

Balance Sheet
as at 31st Dec., 19..

Capital			Fixed Assets			
Capital at 1st Jan., 19..	15000		Freehold Premises		10000	
Add Net Profit	2350		Kitchen Plant	4000		
	17350		Less Depreciation	400	3600	
Less Drawings	500	16850	Restaurant Furniture	2000		
			Less Depreciation	200	1800	
			China and Cutlery	500		
			Less Depreciation	100	400	15800
Current Liabilities			Current Assets			
Creditors	600		Stock		300	
Accrued Light and Heat	50	650	Debtors		300	
			Prepaid Rent and Rates		100	
			Cash at Bank		1000	1700
		17500				17500

Figure 91

Notes on balance sheet

The right-hand (not credit) side of the balance sheet (Figure 91) is known as the 'assets' side. Here it is usual to show separately the fixed and the current assets.

Fixed assets are those which are purchased for retention in the business rather than for re-sale to customers.

Current assets are assets such as cash and assets which, sooner or later, will be converted into cash. Thus, when a debtor pays his debt, a part of the 'debtors' becomes 'cash'. When some provisions are 'converted' into meals and sold for cash, this is a conversion of stock into cash.

It will be appreciated that what constitutes a fixed or a current asset depends primarily on the nature of the business. Furniture in a hotel or restaurant is a fixed asset but in the case of a dealer in furniture it is a current asset.

It is usual to list all the assets in the 'order of liquidity', i.e. according to how easy or how difficult it is to convert the asset concerned into cash. Whether one starts with the most or the least liquid assets does not really matter, though in businesses with a substantial proportion of fixed assets it is common practice to start with the least liquid (premises, equipment, etc.) and end with the most liquid (cash) asset. As most hotel and catering establishments have a large amount of fixed assets, these are usually shown at the top of the balance sheet and are followed by the current assets.

The left-hand side of the balance sheet is known as the 'liabilities' side. Here we have two sections: the 'capital' section and the 'current liabilities' section.

In the capital section we show the capital of the business at the beginning of the accounting period, any additions to the capital (e.g. net profit), any deductions from the capital (e.g. drawings) as well as the result, known as the closing capital —i.e. the capital at the end of the accounting period. The capital of the business is shown on the liabilities side of the balance sheet because it is a debt from the business to the proprietor(s) of the business.

Current liabilities are amounts owing to outsiders which are payable within a few weeks or months of the balance sheet date. Examples of current liabilities are debts owing to the suppliers (trade creditors), those owing in respect of expenses such as light, heat, stationery, wages, etc. (expense creditors), and overdrafts and short-term bank loans.

A debt of a more permanent nature such as a mortgage owing to a building society would be put under the heading of long-term liabilities.

Closing entries In the example given above the trading, profit and loss account was compiled by taking the appropriate figures from the trial balance. In practice, the trading, profit and loss account might, in fact, be compiled in the same manner but, in addition, certain ledger entries would be made.

It will be remembered that the trading, profit and loss account constitutes a part of the system of double entry and that, therefore, no entry should be made in this account without there being a corresponding entry in some other account. Hence, for each and every item entered in this account there must be a corresponding entry in the ledger. Thus, when the purchases are debited in the trading account, the purchases account must be credited. The credit entry in the trading account in respect of sales must have a corresponding debit in the sales account. The debit in the profit and loss account for wages and salaries must have a corresponding credit entry in the wages and salaries account.

All such entries made at the end of an accounting period are known as closing entries and have to be journalized. When the closing entries have been completed, the only balances remaining in the ledger are those in respect of assets and liabilities —balances used in the compilation of the balance sheet. In other words, the effect of the closing entries is to transfer all balances in respect of gains and losses (income and expenditure) to the trading, profit and loss account and to leave in the ledger balances representing assets and liabilities only. A few specimen closing entries are shown in Figure 92.

19..					
Dec.	31	Trading A/c	Dr.	8000	00
		Purchases A/c		8000	00
		Being balance transferred			
"	31	Sales A/c	Dr.	20000	00
		Trading A/c		20000	00
		Being balance transferred			
"	31	Profit and Loss A/c	Dr.	5500	00
		Wages and Salaries A/c		5500	00
		Being balance transferred			

Figure 92

When all the journal entries have been made, the next step is to debit or credit the appropriate accounts in the ledger, completing the double entry in the trading, profit and loss account as shown (Figure 93).

Purchases A/c

various dates	Balance	8000	00	19.. Dec.	31	Trading A/c	8000	00

Sales A/c

19.. Dec.	31	Trading A/c	20000	00	various dates	Balance	20000	00

Wages and Salaries A/c

various dates	Balance	5500	00	19.. Dec.	31	P/L A/c	5500	00

Figure 93

Stock account It may be seen, by reference to the trading account in the example, that at the end of an accounting period it is necessary to show the opening and closing stocks in the trading account in order to arrive at the cost of sales for that year. In the stock account this is completed in two stages, as follows.

First, the opening stock of provisions is debited in the trading account and credited in the stock account, Figure 94. The effect of this entry is to balance the stock account.

19.. Dec.	31	Trading A/c Dr.	400	00		
		Stock A/c			400	00
		Being opening stock transferred				
		to Trading A/c				

Stock A/c

19.. Jan.	1	Balance	b/d	400	00	19.. Dec.	31	Trading A/c	400	00

Figure 94

Second, it is necessary to enter in the stock account the closing stock of provisions as valued at the end of the year. This is shown in Figure 95.

19.. Dec.	31	Stock A/c Dr.	300	00		
		Trading A/c			300	00
		Being stock of provisions as				
		at above date.				

Stock A/c

19.. Jan.	1	Balance	b/d	400	00	19.. Dec.	31	Trading A/c	400	00
Dec.	31	Trading A/c		300	00					

Figure 95

As the stock account has been debited, the correct entry in the trading account is a credit. It is usual, however, to show the closing stock as a deduction on the debit side of the trading account. This has the same effect as if the closing stock were shown as a positive item on the credit side of the trading account.

Adjustments

The object of the profit and loss account is to show the *true* profit or loss for the period under review. That means that the profit and loss account must be credited with *all the income earned* during that year, whether or not the cash in respect of that income has been received; and debited with all the *expenditure incurred*, whether or not the cash in respect of such expenditure has actually been paid out.

Now, it will be appreciated that often income is earned during a particular accounting period and, for one reason or another, is not received until the following accounting period. Similarly, an expense may be incurred towards the end of an accounting period and not actually paid until the following period. As a result, every time a profit and loss account is prepared, certain items of income and expenditure have to be 'adjusted' to correspond with the accounting period.

A hotel may have some investments the income from which may be received after the end of its accounting year. Also, interest on any sums credited to the hotel's deposit account may not be paid by the bank until after the accounting year during which such interest was earned. All such income due but not, for the time being, received must be credited in the profit and loss account. As, at the date of the balance sheet, any such amounts are still owing to the hotel, the parties from whom such income is due are debtors to the hotel. All income due but not yet received must, therefore, be shown in the balance sheet under the heading of current assets. The following example will make this clear.

Example

A hotel has investments amounting to £10 000, producing income at the rate of five per cent per annum. The income is due half-yearly at 30th June and 31st December, the latter being also the end of the hotel's accounting year. Assuming that the second half-yearly instalment of income is not received by the hotel until 5th January next, the entries given in Figure 96 would be found in the ledger of the hotel.

In the hotel's profit and loss account and in the balance sheet the treatment of this investment income would be as shown in Figure 97.

117

Cash Book

	Current Year								
June 30	Investment								
	Income	250	00						
	Following Year								
Jan. 5	Investment								
	Income	250	00						

Investment Income A/c

	Current Year					Current Year			
Dec. 31	P/L A/c	500	00	June 30	Cash		250	00	
				Dec. 31	Balance	c/d	250	00	
		500	00				500	00	
	Following Year				Following Year				
Jan. 1	Balance	b/d	250	00	Jan. 5	Cash		250	00

Figure 96

			(Extract from) Profit and Loss A/c		
			Investment		
			Income	500	00
			(Extract from) Balance Sheet		
			Current Assets		
			Investment		
			Income Due	250	00

Figure 97

Similarly, at the end of each accounting year it will be found that whilst certain expenses have been paid in advance others have been incurred but not yet paid. In the above example the rent and rates are paid in advance (pre-paid) and the light and heat in arrear. The two ledger accounts would be closed as shown in Figure 98.

				Rent and Rates A/c							
various dates		Balance		1700	00	19.. Dec.	31	P/L A/c		1600	00
						"	31	Balance	c/d	100	00
				1700	00					1700	00
19.. Jan.	1	Balance	b/d	100	00						
				Light and Heat A/c							
various dates		Balance		900	00	19.. Dec.	31	P/L A/c		950	00
Dec.	31	Balance	c/d	50	00						
				950	00					950	00
						19.. Jan	1	Balance	b/d	50	00

Figure 98

It should be pointed out that, after the preparation of the profit and loss account, the rent and rates account shows a debit balance and the light and heat account a credit balance. One is an asset and the other a liability and must be shown as such in the balance sheet.

Depreciation

All fixed assets such as premises, furniture, kitchen equipment, china, glass, and cutlery deteriorate in value by wear and tear as well as the passage of time, and at the end of each successive accounting period the value of each asset is less and less.

The loss in the value of an asset is known as depreciation and must be debited in the profit and loss account of the business. When, for example, a hotel buys furniture for £1 000, and it is estimated that it will last ten years, the cost of the furniture to the hotel is £100 p.a. and this must be debited in its profit and loss account.

There are three main methods of depreciation:

(1) The fixed instalment method, under which the annual charge for depreciation is calculated by dividing the initial cost of the asset by the estimated life of the asset. For example, when a lease of premises for ten years is purchased for £10 000, the amount of depreciation to be charged to profit and loss account is £1 000 p.a.

(2) The reducing balance method, under which the charge for depreciation is expressed as a percentage of the book value of the asset at the beginning of each accounting year. For example, when an asset is purchased for £10 000 and it is decided to depreciate it at the rate of ten per cent, the depreciation debited in the profit and loss account would be:

Initial cost of asset	£10 000
Year I depreciation (10% of £10 000)	1 000
Book value of asset, beginning of year II	9 000
Year II depreciation (10% of £9 000)	900
Book value of asset, beginning of year III	8 100
Year III depreciation (10% of £8 100)	810
Book value of asset, beginning of year IV	£7 290

(3) The revaluation method, which is used for small items of equipment such as china, cutlery, linen, and glass. The depreciation to be written off is based on periodical inventories. The amount to be debited to the profit and loss account is the decrease in the value of such asset, as shown by the inventories. For example, when the value of china at the beginning of a year is £500 and according to the inventory at the end of the year £400, the amount that should be debited in the profit and loss account is £100.

Any ledger entries in respect of depreciation must be journalized and Figure 99 shows the journal and ledger entries in respect of the kitchen plant account in the

Figure 99

The value of the asset at the beginning of the accounting period, the depreciation written off, and the net value of the asset at the end of the accounting period are shown in the balance sheet.

Capital, net profit and drawings

From the balance sheet given in the example it may be seen that the balance of the proprietor's capital account increased during the year covered by the final accounts by £1 850. Any increase or decrease in the amount of the capital must be reflected by appropriate entries in the capital account. At the end of each accounting year it is, therefore, necessary to:

(a) credit in the capital account any profit that has been made by the business; the profit belongs to the proprietor and his capital must be increased accordingly. If a business makes a net loss then this must, of course, be debited in the capital account.

(b) debit in the capital account any drawings of the proprietor, whether in cash or in goods.

Any amount of cash withdrawn by the owner of a business would, during the course of the year, be credited in the cash book and debited in his drawings account. Any goods taken by him for private consumption would be credited in the purchases account and debited in the drawings account. The balance of the drawings account would then be transferred to the capital account, as shown in Figure 100.

Capital A/c

19..					19..				
Dec.	31	Drawings	500	00	Jan.	1	Balance	b/d	15000 00
"	31	Balance	c/d	16850 00	"	31	N. Profit		2350 00
			17350 00						17350 00
					19..				
					Jan.	1	Balance	b/d	16850 00

Drawings A/c

					19..				
Various dates	Balance		500 00	Dec.	31	Capital A/c		500 00

Figure 100

Problems   **1** Explain what you understand by gross profit and net profit.

2 Arrange the following assets in the order of liquidity, starting with the least liquid asset: debtors; furniture, china and cutlery; premises; kitchen plant; and cash at bank.

3 Distinguish clearly between fixed assets and current assets. State which of the following are fixed and which are current: leasehold premises; cash at bank; cutlery and utensils; restaurant furniture; banqueting debtors; glass and linen; and liquor stocks.

4 Show the necessary journal and ledger closing entries in respect of the following balances:

(a)	Purchases account	£8 650
(b)	Sales account	17 450
(c)	Opening stock	250
(d)	Closing stock	300
(e)	Wages account	3 750

5 Explain why it is necessary to 'adjust' certain items of income and expenditure when preparing a trading, profit and loss account.

6 What do you understand by 'depreciation'? What are the main methods of depreciation?

7 On 1st January, 1971, a catering company purchased heavy kitchen equipment, having an estimated working life of ten years, for £5 000. It was proposed to depreciate the equipment by the fixed instalment method.

Show the kitchen equipment account as it would appear in the ledger of the company at the end of 1974, balancing it at the end of each year. Show also the relevant extracts from the company's balance sheet at the end of 1972, 1973, and 1974.

8 The following balances were extracted from the ledger of Nix Restaurant, at 31st December, 19...

	£	£
Capital		1 000
Stock, 1 January, 19..	75	
Wages and salaries	500	
Rent	100	
Sales		2 000
Purchases	1 000	
Insurance	20	
Gas and electricity	50	
Kitchen utensils	150	
Restaurant furniture	400	
Creditors		200
Postage and telephone	30	
Cutlery and china	100	
Kitchen equipment	500	
Cash at bank	275	
	£3 200	£3 200

You are required to prepare the restaurant's trading, profit and loss account for the year ended 31st December, 19. ., and a balance sheet as at that date. Take the following additional information into account.

(a) The stock of provisions at 31st December, 19. ., was valued at £50.

(b) Insurance paid in advance amounted to £5, and gas and electricity due but unpaid amounted to £15.

(c) Provide for depreciation as follows: kitchen equipment £50; restaurant furniture 10%; kitchen utensils and china and cutlery were revalued at £120 and £80 respectively.

9 The following trial balance was extracted from the books of the Crown Restaurant at 30th June, 19. ... Prepare the restaurant's trading, profit and loss account for the year ended 30th June, 19. ., and a balance sheet as at that date.

	£	£
Purchases and sales	10 000	23 500
Stock on 1st July, 19. .	650	
Capital		20 000
Trade creditors		800
Rent and rates	450	
Banqueting debtors	850	
Wages and salaries	4 975	
Light and heat	775	
Repairs and replacements	390	
Furniture	1 900	
Kitchen plant	2 200	
China, glass, and cutlery	830	
Drawings	155	
Cash at bank	175	
Leasehold premises	21 000	
Discounts received		50
	£44 350	£44 350

Take the following additional information into account:

(a) The closing stock of provisions was valued at £700.

(b) Depreciate leasehold premises by £500; kitchen plant by 10%; furniture by £150; china, glass, and cutlery were valued at £700.

(c) Light and heat due at 30th June, 19. ., but unpaid amounted to £75.

(d) Of the rent and rates £50 was paid in respect of the following accounting period.

Note: Discounts received, £50, are a gain and should be credited to the profit and loss account.

10 From the following trial balance prepare the trading, profit and loss account for the year ended 31st December, 19 . ., and a balance sheet as at that date.

	£	£
Capital		15 000
Gas and electricity	890	
Rent and rates	950	
Stock, 1st January, 19 . .	310	
Discounts received		105
China and glass	610	
Purchases	9 230	
Freehold premises	11 000	
Purchases returns		50
Printing and stationery	315	
Furniture	1 250	
Cash in hand	10	
Creditors		595
Wages and salaries	5 620	
Postage and telephone	210	
Drawings	850	
Sales		21 610
Kitchen equipment	2 400	
Cash at bank	3 715	
	£37 360	£37 360

Take the following additional information into account:

(a) The stock of provisions at 31st December, 19 . ., was valued at £290.

(b) The stock of unused stationery was valued at £15.

(c) Rates due but unpaid amounted to £50.

(d) Depreciate kitchen equipment by 12%; furniture by 10%; and china and glass by £110.

CHAPTER 10

Departmental accounts

An important practical aspect of book-keeping in the hotel and catering industry is the keeping of analytical books or departmental accounts.

Departmental accounts are a method of book-keeping and accounting the purpose of which is to find how much profit (or loss) has been made by each section or department of a business. In this context 'department' means a revenue-producing (selling) department as, clearly, trading results cannot be obtained for non-revenue producing departments such as wash-up, stores, or reception.

In a business consisting of several revenue-producing departments it is, obviously, necessary to find the profit or loss made by each department. Otherwise the fact that one or more departments are operating at a loss might not be disclosed. The position might be as shown below:

A.B.C. CATERING CO.
Statement of departmental results

	Dept. A	Dept. B	Dept. C	TOTAL
Sales	£10 000	£20 000	£25 000	£55 000
Less costs	6 000	14 000	26 000	46 000
+profit/ −loss	+£4 000	+£6 000	−£1 000	+£9 000

It will be realized that in the vast majority of hotel and catering establishments it is possible in each case to distinguish several revenue-producing departments. Thus in hotels there are accommodation, food, drink, and other sales. Food and drink sales are often sub-divided into banqueting, dining-room, grill room and other departments. In many restaurants it will be found that the total turnover may clearly be separated into food sales, drink sales, and other (sundry) sales. In industrial and institutional catering it is also possible to divide the turnover into appropriate departments and, in this way, to arrive at a separate trading result for each department.

Book-keeping records

In order to achieve the above end, suitably analysed subsidiary books and ledger accounts (known as analytical books) must be kept.

It is usual in most hotel and catering establishments to arrive at a separate figure of gross profit for each department and to debit all expenses such as wages, salaries, rent, and rates against the total of the departmental gross profits. Where that is so, it is only necessary to keep analytical books for purchases, sales, and stocks. All other accounts (wages, salaries, rent, rates, etc.) are then kept in the usual manner and do not need to be analysed.

Example In a restaurant selling food, drink and cigarettes, the purchases day book would be analysed as shown in Figure 101.

Purchases Day Book

Date		F	Total	Food	Drink	Cigarettes
19..						
Jan 1	A.B. Brown & Co. Ltd.		26:00	26.00		
" 2	Irish Whiskey Ltd.		34.00		34.00	
" 3	N.O. Nicotine Ltd.		10.00			10.00
" 4	B.A. Grocer & Sons Ltd.		12.00	12.00		
" 31	Trans to Purchases A/c		1600.00	1100.00	400.00	100.00

Figure 101

From the purchases day book the periodical totals would be posted to an analysed purchases account as shown in Figure 102.

Purchases A/c

Date		Total	Food	Drink	Cigs.	Date		Total	Food	Drink	Cigs.
19..											
Jan 15	Cash	20	20								
" 31	Sundries	1600	1100	400	100						

Figure 102

Similarly, the sales of the restaurant would have to be analysed in the same manner. At the end of each day the restaurant's cash and credit sales would be analysed under the headings: food, drink, and cigarettes. Cash sales would be recorded as in Figure 103.

Cash Book

Date		Detail	Bank	Date		Detail	Bank
19.. Jan 1	Balance b/d		1 000	19.. Jan.15	Purchases(Food)		20
" 2	Sales - Food	200					
	Drink	100					
	Cigs.	50	350				

Figure 103

The credit sales would be entered in an analysed restaurant sales book (Figure 104) the totals of which would be posted to the sales account, as shown in Figure 105.

Restaurant Sales Book

Date		F	Total	Food	Drink	Cigarettes
19.. Jan. 1	Essex Motors Ltd.		15	10	5	
" 2	Capt. A. V. Smart		10	7	2	1
" 3	Utopian Projects Ltd.		50	35	10	5
	etc.					
" 31	Trans. to Sales A/c		900	500	320	80

Figure 104

127

Sales A/c

Date		Total	Food	Drink	Cigs	Date		Total	Food	Drink	Cigs
						19-- Jan 2	Cash	350	200	100	50
							etc				
						" 31	Sundries	900	500	320	80

Figure 105

Finally, an analysed stock account would have to be kept. This would also have appropriate columns for the various stocks kept by the restaurant, Figure 106.

Stock A/c

Date		Total	Food	Drink	Cigs	Date		Total	Food	Drink	Cigs
19-- Jan 1	Balances b/d	550	200	300	50						

Figure 106

Where a system of analysed records is kept on the above lines, it is possible at the end of each accounting period to ascertain the gross profit (or gross loss) of each department.

There are some businesses, however, which go a stage further and analyse expenses such as wages, salaries, lighting, heating, etc., and arrive at a figure of net profit (or net loss) for each department. Where that is done, many more analytical records must be kept, and expenses which are paid on behalf of the business as a whole (e.g. rent, rates, depreciation of premises) must be apportioned to the various departments on some fair basis.

Departmental trading account

A departmental trading account is prepared in very much the same way as indicated in the previous chapter, except that it is necessary to provide in it a separate column for each revenue-producing department.

Trading, Profit and Loss A/c
for year ending 31st Dec., 19..

	Food	Drink	Cigs.	Total		Food	Drink	Cigs	Total
Opening Stocks	200	300	50	550	Sales	17100	11250	900	29250
Purchases	8000	5000	800	13800					
	8200	5300	850	14350					
Less closing Stocks	150	250	40	440					
Cost of Sales	8050	5050	810	13910					
Gross Profit c/d	9050	6200	90	15340					
	17100	11250	900	29250		17100	11250	900	29250
Wages and Salaries				7550	Gross Profit b/d				15340
Rent and Rates				1830	Discounts received				160
Lighting and Heating				890					
Repairs and Replacements				630					
Depreciation				1240					
Postage and Stationery				310					
Miscellaneous Expenses				200					
N. Profit-trans. to Capital A/c				2850					
				15500					15500

Figure 107

A specimen departmental trading account and a profit and loss account are given in Figure 107.

As may be seen from the above trading, profit and loss account, a departmental trading account helps to keep a check on the gross profit margin of each department.

The balance sheet is not affected by departmental accounts, except that the stocks kept in the various departments may be shown separately under the heading of current assets.

Problems   1 Describe the objects and advantages of departmental accounts.

2 The following trial balance was extracted from the books of the London Catering Co. at 1st January, 19...

	£	£
Capital		5 000
Cash at bank	1 040	
Freehold premises	3 650	
Petty cash	10	
Creditors: X. L. Groceries Ltd		100
U. K. Tobacco Co.		50
O. K. Provisions Ltd		50
Stocks: food	200	
cigarettes	50	
China and cutlery	250	
	£5 200	£5 200

The transactions of the company in January were:

			£
January	1	Withdrawn from bank for petty cash	£10
„	3	Received invoices from: U. K. Tobacco Co.	30
		O. K. Provisions Ltd	75
		X. L. Groceries Ltd	35
„	7	Paid out of petty cash: travelling expenses	2
		cleaning materials	1
		vegetables	3
„	10	Purchased groceries for cash	95
„	13	Received credit notes from: U. K. Tobacco Co.	5
		O. K. Provisions Ltd	4
„	15	Banked cash sales: meals	150
		cigarettes	35
„	18	Purchased cutlery on credit from Catering Supplies Ltd	50
„	21	Received invoices from: X. L. Groceries Ltd	75
		U. K. Tobacco Co.	25
		O. K. Provisions Ltd	55
„	21	Withdrew from bank for private use	45
„	24	Banked cash sales: meals	175
		cigarettes	40
„	25	Received credit note from X. L. Groceries Ltd	7
„	27	Paid account of X. L. Groceries Ltd, as at 1st January	
„	31	Paid out of petty cash: travelling expenses	3
		fruit	2

Record the above transactions in appropriate books, extract a trial balance as at 31st January, 19.., and balance the cash book, petty cash book and the accounts of suppliers.

3 The following balances appeared in Alan West's ledger at 30th November, 19...

	£	£
Stocks: food	72	
wines and spirits	105	
tobaccos	33	
Sales: food		4 550
wines and spirits		1 803
tobaccos		226
Purchases: food	2 204	
wines and spirits	825	
tobaccos	203	
Wages and salaries	1 991	
Capital		5 000
Creditors: London Grocers Ltd		20
D. C. Butcher		25
City Wine Co.		27
London Tobacco Co.		19
Advertising	420	
Drawings	525	
Fuel and light	316	
Cash at bank	253	
Petty cash	10	
Repairs and replacements	198	
Restaurant furniture	450	
China, linen, and cutlery	150	
Miscellaneous expenses	21	
Leasehold premises	3 750	
Rates	65	
Discount received		41
Debtors: V. S. Dining Club	10	
Empire Chemicals Ltd	55	
The '62 Society	25	
Ruritanian Airways	30	
	£11 711	£11 711

You are required to open the necessary books and record West's transactions in December, which were as follows:

December	1	Credit purchases: London Grocers Ltd				£52
		D. C. Butcher				47
		London Tobacco Co.				12
		City Wine Co.				108
,,	4	Paid for electricity				51
,,	7	Paid wages and salaries				47
,,	8	Banked cash sales: food				149
		wines and spirits				76
		tobaccos				10
,,	9	Credit sales:				
			Food	*W. & S.*	*Tob.*	
		The '62 Society	£7	£2	£1	10
		V.C. Dining Club	3	3	–	6
		Ruritanian Airways	4	2	1	7
,,	11	Credit purchases: London Grocers Ltd				41
		D. C. Butcher				12
		City Wine Co.				55

(continued)

			Food	W. & S.	Tob.	
December	13	Withdrew from bank for private use				£30
,,	15	Received credit note from D. C. Butcher				3
,,	17	Banked cash sales: food				205
		wines and spirits				73
		tobaccos				5
,,	18	Credit sales:				
		Empire Chemicals Ltd	£17	£5	£1	23
		V.C. Dining Club	3	5	2	10
		The '62 Society	6	3	1	10
,,	19	Paid wages and salaries				73
,,	21	Credit purchases: London Tobacco Co.				9
		City Wine Co.				67
		London Grocers Ltd				56
		D. C. Butcher				41
,,	22	Paid the following suppliers' accounts as at 30th November, 19. . :				
		London Grocers Ltd — cash disc. £1				
		D. C. Butcher ,, ,, 2				
		City Wine Co. ,, ,, 1				
		London Tobacco Co. ,, ,, Nil				
,,	24	Paid wages and salaries				51
,,	24	Received credit note from City Wine Co.				6
,,	25	Petty cash payments: stationery				1
		fruit and vegetables				2
		postage stamps				1
,,	26	Banked cash sales: food				59
		wines and spirits				67
		tobaccos				9
,,	27	The '62 Society and Empire Chemicals Ltd paid their accounts as at 30th November, 19. .				
,,	28	Paid for advertising				60
,,	28	Paid for gas				35
,,	29	Credit sales:				
		Ruritanian Airways	£6	£2	£1	9
		V.C. Dining Club	20	3	–	23
		Empire Chemicals Ltd	3	6	1	10
,,	30	Paid wages and salaries				60
,,	31	Petty cash payments: stationery				1
		fruit				2
		postage stamps				1
,,	31	Withdrew from bank for private use				20

Extract West's trial balance as at 31st December, 19. ., and balance the cash book, petty cash book and all personal accounts.

4 The following balances appeared in the books of the Hypothetical Restaurant at 31st December, 19... You are required to prepare the trading, profit and loss account of the restaurant for the year ended 31st December, 19...

Sales: meals	£38 450
liquors	23 475
tobaccos	1 220
Stocks, 1st January, 19..: food	300
liquors	480
tobaccos	40
Purchases: food	18 950
liquors	11 830
tobaccos	1 020
Repairs and renewals	1 340
Postage and telephone	640
Printing and stationery	420
Rent and rates	3 425
Wages and salaries	16 840
Gas and electricity	1 490
Sundry expenses	350

The stocks of the restaurant at 31st December, 19.., were valued as follows: food £325, liquors £460, tobaccos £80. Gas and electricity due but unpaid amounted to £120.

5 The following balances were extracted from the books of a catering establishment at 30th June, 19...

	£	£
Capital		10 000
Cash at bank	2 293	
Wages and salaries	2 976	
Fuel and light	716	
Sales: meals		9 005
wines, spirits, etc.		3 605
cigarettes		452
Advertising	845	
Petty cash	15	
Leasehold premises	7 500	
Creditors		157
Renewals and replacements	412	
Drawings	550	
China, linen, and cutlery	200	
Discounts received		141
Rates	130	
Restaurant furniture	800	
Miscellaneous expenses	45	
Stocks, 1st July, 19..: food	145	
wines, spirits, etc.	210	
cigarettes	65	
Purchases: food	4 403	
wines, spirits, etc.	1 649	
cigarettes	406	
	£23 360	£23 360

133

You are required to prepare a trading, profit and loss account for the year ended 30th June, 19 . ., and a balance sheet as at that date. The following notes should be taken into account:

(a) Stocks at 30th June, 19 . ., were valued as follows: food, £165; wines, spirits etc., £260; cigarettes, £80.

(b) Provide for depreciation as follows: leasehold premises, £300; restaurant furniture, 10%. China, linen, and cutlery were revalued at £160.

(c) Fuel and light due but not paid amounted to £34.

(d) Rates paid in advance amounted to £20.

CHAPTER 11

Other forms of ownership

The main objective of chapter 9 was to introduce the student to the construction of simple final accounts. The subject-matter of that chapter related to one particular form of ownership, viz. the sole trader.

Whilst there are numerous sole traders engaged in the hotel and catering industry, there are, however, very many establishments where the form of ownership is different. Thus there are many establishments which are run not primarily to earn a profit but mainly for welfare reasons, e.g. industrial canteens. Similarly, there are many hotel and catering establishments which belong to partners or limited companies. Hence, it is appropriate even in an introductory volume on accounting to give a brief outline of these other types of business organization.

Non-profit making bodies

Examples of non-profit making bodies are sports clubs, charities, political and religious institutions, professional bodies, etc. The main objective of all those is to promote their aims and not to earn profits.

The final accounts of such bodies are prepared as explained in chapter 9. What is rather different about these accounts is, in the main, the terminology used.

What was described in chapter 9 as the profit and loss account is in non-profit making bodies described as the 'income and expenditure account'. The income and expenditure account is credited with all income earned (e.g. subscriptions, entrance fees, donations received, catering receipts, etc.) and debited with all expenses incurred. As with the profit and loss account, adjustments for pre-payments and accruals are necessary.

A credit balance on the income and expenditure account is described as 'net surplus' or 'excess of income over expenditure'. A debit balance on the income and expenditure account is described as 'not deficit' or 'excess of expenditure over income'.

The balance sheet of a non-profit making body is prepared in the same way as the balance sheet of the sole trader. What in the case of the sole trader was described as 'capital' is sometimes referred to as 'accumulated fund' or 'capital fund'.

A specimen example of final accounts of a non-profit making body is given in Figures 108, 109, 110.

Partnerships

A partnership is an association of at least two but typically several persons, who carry on a business with a view to profit. Clearly, this form of business ownership has certain advantages over the sole trader type of business. Other things being equal, several persons can raise more capital than one person. Also, this form of ownership enables the partners to specialise in various aspects or departments of the business. Thus one of the partners may take charge of accounts and control, another partner may take charge of food and beverage operations, whilst the third partner may act as reception manager.

It is essential that, before a partnership is entered into, there is a proper Partnership Agreement drawn up by the partners. This will deal with a variety of matters, such as: how much capital is to be contributed by each partner; how profits and losses are to be shared; how frequently accounts should be drawn up, etc.

Catering Account
for year ended 31st Dec., 19..

Opening Stock	50	Sales	1425
Add Purchases	900		
	950		
Less Closing Stock	100		
Cost of Sales	850		
Catering Wages	160		
Catering Profit c/d	415		
	£1 425		£1 425

Figure 108

Income and Expenditure Account
for year ended 31st Dec., 19..

Rent	200	Catering Profit b/d	415
Printing and Stationery	35	Subscriptions	750
Postage and Telephone	25	Donations	25
Sec. Honorarium	50	Sundry Receipts	70
Wages	250		
Cleaning	30		
Repairs	10		
Depreciation	80		
Prizes	50		
Net Surplus	530		
	£1 260		£1 260

Figure 109

Balance Sheet
as at 31st Dec., 19..

Accumulated Fund			Fixed Assets		
Balance on 1st Jan., 19..	2700		Leasehold	2500	
Add Net Surplus	530	3230	Less Depreciation	50	2450
			Furniture	100	
			Less Depreciation	10	90
			Games Equipment	200	2740
Current Liabilities			Current Assets		
Refreshment Creditors		150	Stock of Refreshments	100	
			Subscriptions Due	25	
			Cash at Bank	515	640
		£3380			£3380

Figure 110

Partnerships
(cont.)

In general the accounts of a partnership do not differ from those of other types of business. It is still necessary to keep the same subsidiary books and ledger accounts as explained in the earlier chapters. The main changes which are introduced here arise from the fact that the capital of the business has been contributed by two or more persons and that, in consequence, the net profit or loss has to be shared between the proprietors. It is, therefore, necessary to have a separate capital account for each partner.

In the case of the sole trader the whole of the net profit or loss is transferred direct from the profit and loss account to the capital account. In a partnership the net profit or net loss is divided between the partners (in accordance with the partnership agreement) in what is known as the 'appropriation account'. This is a continuation of the profit and loss account.

Example
A and B are proprietors of the Metropolitan Hotel. Their capitals on 1st January, 19.. were: A—£4 000; B—£3 000. During the year ended 31st December, 19.. their drawings amounted to £100 and £400 respectively, and the net profit for the year was £2 050.

Prepare the hotel's appropriation account for the year ended 31st December, 19.., and the partners' capital accounts as at that date, taking the following notes into account:

(a) partners are entitled to interest on their capitals at the rate of 5 per cent per annum;

(b) partners are entitled to salaries as follows: A—£600; B—£700;

(c) the balance of profit or loss is to be shared by them equally.

137

Appropriation Account
for the year ended 31st Dec., 19..

Interest on Capitals:			Net Profit b/d	2 050
A 200				
B 150	350			
Salaries:				
A 600				
B 700	1300			
Net Profit:				
A 200				
B 200	400			
	2 050			2 050

Figure 111

Capital A/c — A

19..					19..					
Dec.	31	Drawings		100 00	Jan.	1	Balance	b/d	4000	00
-	31	Balance	c/d	4900 00	Dec.	31	Int. on Capital		200	00
					"	31	Salary		600	00
					"	31	Net Profit		200	00
				5 000 00					5000	00
					Jan.	1	Balance	b/d	4900	00

Capital A/c — B.

19..					19..					
Dec.	31	Drawings		400 00	Jan.	1	Balance	b/d	3000	00
"	31	Balance	c/d	3650 00	Dec.	31	Int. on Capital		150	00
					"	31	Salary		700	00
					"	31	Net Profit		200	00
				4050 00					4050	00
					19..					
					Jan.	1	Balance	b/d	3 650	00

Figure 112

The balance sheet of the partnership would then be drawn up as in the case of the sole trader, except that particulars of the capital accounts would be given separately for partner A and partner B.

Limited companies

A limited company is known as such because the proprietors (shareholders) of the company have what is known as 'limited liability' for the debts of the business. Generally, in other types of business the proprietors have full (unlimited) liability for debts incurred by the business and this extends even to property they own elsewhere. Thus a partner may have to sell his private possessions to pay the debts of the partnership. A shareholder is in a privileged position. Once he has paid in full for his shares, he cannot be asked for any further contribution whatever the debts of the company.

This, clearly, is an important advantage for this particular type of business organization, and one of the reasons for the rapid growth of limited companies, both in the hotel and catering industry and elsewhere. Some limited companies have thousands of shareholders and are, as a result, able to raise very substantial sums of money as capital. Indeed, without this form of business ownership large-scale business organizations would have been impossible.

A limited company raises its capital by issuing (selling) shares and sometimes also debentures. Ordinary shares, which are the most common, have no special rights. Dividends paid on these shares tend to vary in accordance with profits earned. In a lean year there may be no ordinary dividend paid at all; when profits are high dividends on ordinary shares may be very substantial. Preference shareholders are entitled to a fixed dividend and this has to be paid before any dividend is paid on the ordinary shares. They thus have a right of preference over ordinary shareholders. Debentures are rather different. A debenture is a loan to the company which attracts a fixed rate of interest; debentures are, therefore, not regarded as part of the capital of the limited company. A debenture holder is, therefore, a creditor and not a part-proprietor of the company. A dividend may only be paid if there is a profit; interest on debentures has to be paid even when losses are incurred by the company.

When a company issues shares the entries are:

Dr—Cash Book
Cr—Share Capital A/c

Example

The London Hotel Co. Ltd, has issued 10 000 ordinary shares of £1 each and 10 000 8% preference shares of £1 each. Both were paid in full on application. The entries in the books of the company would appear as in Figure 113.

Let us assume that immediately after the receipt of the £20 000 the company spent the following amounts:

Land and buildings	£12 000
Kitchen plant	3 000
Furniture	3 000
Food stocks	1 000
Total	£19 000

The balance sheet of the company would then appear as in Figure 114.

139

		Cash Book.				
...	.. Ord. Shares	10000	00			
...	.. 8% Pref. Shares	10000	00			
		Ordinary Shares A/c				
		...	.. Cash	10000	00
		8% Preference Shares A/c				
		...	.. Cash	10000	00

Figure 113

Balance Sheet
as at .....

Capital		Fixed Assets.		
10000 Ordinary Shares of £1 each	10000	Land and Buildings	12000	
10000 8% Pref. Shares of £1 each	10000	Kitchen Plant	3000	
		Furniture	3000	18000
		Current Assets.		
		Food Stocks	1000	
		Cash at Bank	1000	2000
	£ 20000			£ 20000

Figure 114

The profits earned by a limited company have to satisfy several claims. Some of the profit will be needed to discharge the tax liabilities of the company; some of it will be used to pay dividends. If there is some profit still left, some or all of it may be transferred to reserve (i.e. put aside for unspecified future needs) and a certain amount may be carried forward to the next accounting period. The appropriation or division of the total net profit of a limited company is made in an appropriation account, which is an extension of the profit and loss account. An example is given below.

Appropriation Account for year ended		Net Profit	
Taxation	8 000	Net Profit	20 000
Ordinary Dividend	6 000		
Preference Dividend	2 000		
General Reserve	3 000		
Balance c/f.	1 000		
	20 000		20 000

Figure 115

Problems
1 What do you understand by:
(a) income and expenditure account;
(b) net surplus;
(c) net deficit;
(d) capital fund;
(e) accumulated fund?

2 Write short, explanatory notes on:
(a) partnership agreement;
(b) appropriation account.

3 What are the main differences between the limited company and the partnership?

4 The Instant Hotel Co. Ltd., has issued 20 000 ordinary shares of £1 each and 20 000 8% preference shares of £1 each. Immediately after the receipt of the cash due from shareholders, the company purchased the following:

Freehold premises	£25 000
Furniture	5 000
Kitchen plant	5 000
China and Cutlery	2 000
Food stocks	1 000

Show the balance sheet of the company after the completion of the above transactions.

5 The proprietors of the Black Tulip Hotel are A.B. and C.D. Their capitals are: A.B.—£6 000; C.D.—£2 500. They share profits and losses as follows:

(a) A.B. is to receive a salary of £600 per annum;

(b) C.D. is to receive a salary of £500 per annum;

(c) Partners are entitled to interest on their capitals at the rate of 4 per cent;

(d) The remaining profits are to be shared in the ratio: A.B. $\frac{6}{10}$; C.D. $\frac{4}{10}$.

Calculate the total amount due to each partner at the end of 19.., when the net profit of the hotel was £3,550.

Index